I0823011

TO CATCH A FISH

....

TO CATCH A FISH

....

Essays on the Joy, Frustration, Curiosity, and Allure of Fishing

MARK KURLANSKY

Illustrations by BRI DOSTIE

CONTENTS

PART TWO: WHAT DO I DO WITH IT NOW?

PART THREE: FISHING BY THE BOOK

INTRODUCTION

THE INTRIGUE

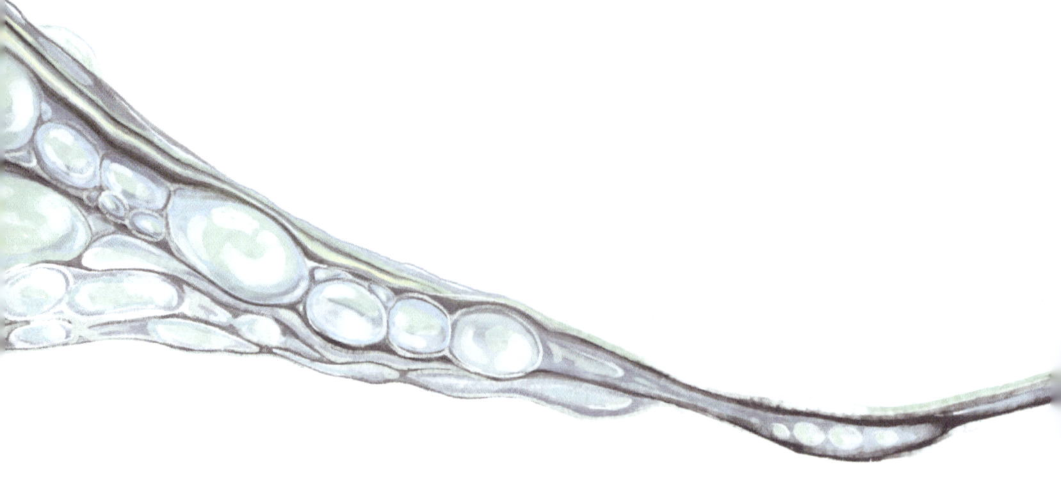

I have been fishing for as long as I can remember . . . and writing about it almost as long. I have caught bluefish and stripers in New England; trout in Idaho, New York, and Spain; barracuda in Senegal's winding Saloum River; salmon in Alaska, Scotland, Japan, and Russia; and other fish in other places. When I go somewhere, I look for a fishing opportunity. When I look at water—a river, a stretch of ocean, a lake, or even a pond—I always wonder what fish are there and what they are eating. Some of us find a connection with nature by chasing deer in forests or watching birds in flight. Fishing connects us with a mysterious side of nature that we cannot—at first glance—see. That is part of the attraction: We are trying to outsmart unseen wildlife. Though we cannot see them, we try to predict their movements; it's like hunting lions in the dark. I'm drawn to the intrigue of trying to penetrate an unknown world. It is a complicated world, difficult to understand, with an order to it and natural laws.

PART ONE

CATCHING FISH

MY FIRST FISH

I caught my first fish when I was a small boy. Even then, when I looked at a body of water, I wondered about the life below. There was a nearby park with a pond about four feet deep and a small waterfall. I liked to sit by the waterfall and read. But my mind would wander to the depths of the pond.

For a little money, pocket change, I bought a fishhook, a small lead weight, and some fishing line. I thought about just using string but realized that the fish would see it. I tied the hook to the line and the weight a little farther up. I tied the other 10 feet of line to the tip of a dead, fallen branch. I dug up an earthworm in my parents' garden and cut it in two so I would have two slithering earthworms for bait. Nothing could have been further from my thoughts than the plight of earthworms! I just wanted to catch a fish.

I put one of the worms on the hook and dropped it in the pond. I felt a tug on my arm. If you've fished, you know—nothing is more exciting. I have caught fish of many different types and sizes. They all pull with surprising strength. Whatever the size, it's exhilarating to feel the strength of a wild animal fighting you. This first one was not very big, and its tug was not very powerful. But my arm wasn't very big in those days, either.

I whipped the stick up and landed a bright little sunfish on the bank. I caught a second one with the other half worm.

I took them home, but my mother refused to cook them.

Undeterred, I had a new idea for the next day. One of the fish had claw marks on its side. There was something down there trying to catch the same fish I did.

The next day I brought one of the rejected sunfish back to the pond. It was now looking less appealing to me, but I thought it might appeal to a hungrier creature.

I tied it on the line with two of the small lead weights and dragged it along the bottom of the pond. When I felt a jerk on the line, I quickly flipped it to the bank and saw that the sunfish now had a pink-and-gray crayfish stubbornly hanging on with its claws. With this one sunfish I caught three crayfish—a better bargain than the two sunfish I had caught with two half worms.

I took them home in my rusty coffee can, but my mother refused to cook these, too.

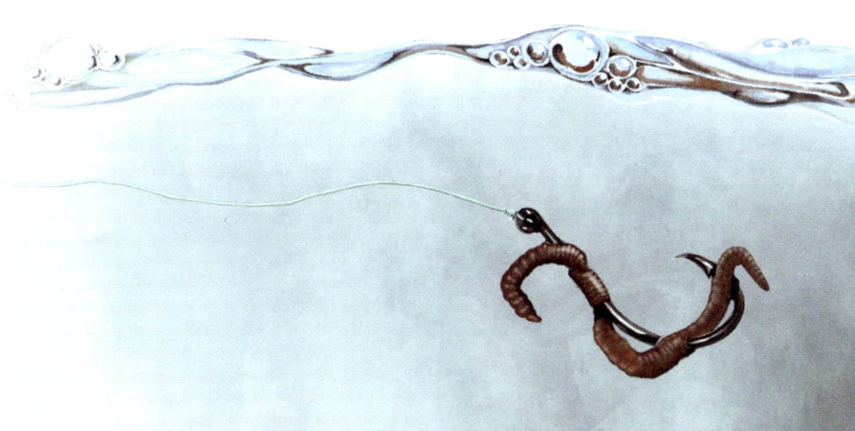

THE SECRET TO CATCHING FISH

We can catch fish because they are hungry much of the time. If there were a thought bubble floating over a fish's head, it would probably read, "Food! Food! I want some food!" Finding food is one of the main activities in a fish's life.

To catch a fish you have to know what they like to eat and what time of day is mealtime. It is often said that early morning is the best time to catch fish, but this is not always true. Sunset is often a good time. Midday sometimes works, depending on the weather. Fish do not have eyelids,

Sunfish lurk in the shade along the banks of a river.

and so they do not like strong sunlight. In a river you will find them in the shade along the banks. In the Dominican Republic commercial fishers sometimes place a palm tree floating upright attached to a buoy in the middle of the ocean. Fish are attracted to the shade of the tree.

Fish are picky about their food. Some eat worms, some smaller fish, some frogs, some mice, some insects. But you have to know what kind of fish or frog or fly they like to eat, and it may depend on the season or even the lighting. You also have to move that food through the water in a believable way and place it where the fish like to swim. It may be a current, a deep trench, or a shallow shelf. Or a place where something that fish like to eat is hatching. There are many reasons why a fish will pick a certain place in the water, just as a mammal has a favorite spot in the forest.

But sometimes all you have to do is arouse the fish's curiosity with a certain kind of movement, a bright color, or a metallic shine.

To catch a fish you have to think like a fish—like the particular fish you're after. That is why fishing is fun—the brain contest (followed by the brawn contest). The novelist John Steinbeck once wrote, "Anyone who pits his intelligence against a fish and loses has it coming."

But don't sell fish short. They are not only fast, graceful, and beautiful, they are cunning. Most of the time you will lose. That is why winning is fun. It's like playing baseball. If you get a hit a third of the time, you are a star. The rarity is why getting a hit feels so good. And the fish always has the home-field advantage.

OFFERING NOTHING: FISHING WITHOUT BAIT

You can catch some types of fish with no bait and no equipment. All you need is speed and skill. For example, "tickling" trout is a technique that's been around for a few thousand years. You will find mention of it in ancient Greek texts; Shakespeare and Mark Twain talk about this fishing technique, too.

Relentless predators as we humans are, we've discovered that trout are particularly susceptible to tickling. And though we say "tickling," trout are not really ticklish.

To tickle a trout, I might sneak up on one resting on a rock ledge and carefully slip a hand underneath, rubbing the trout's belly until it becomes still and relaxed; then, in a flick of the wrist, I toss it to the bank. Actually, I have never accomplished this amazing feat, though I have tried and seen it done.

"Noodling" for catfish is a similar technique, but it is more painful. You offer yourself as bait. This is appealing because buying bait or lures is one of the greatest expenses of fishing.

To noodle, one must wiggle a finger—resembling a wet noodle—in the water. The catfish chomps onto the dangled finger, which is yanked up out of the water, catfish in tow. This fishing style is also called grabbling, hogging, or hand-fishing. The hard part of this approach: Catfish are larger than trout. And their teeth are sharp.

Jigging, like these other baitless approaches, is extremely difficult. It is a technique used by highly skilled commercial fishers. I tried it once with inshore cod fishermen in Newfoundland. These were the most skilled fishers I have ever had the privilege of fishing with, and they seemed to share a mystical understanding of the bottom-dwelling codfish.

To jig, cod fishers hold a line in their hands with no rod or reel and lean over the rails of their small, inshore skiffs (a skiff is a small boat that fishes close to land). They lower a sharp, heavily weighted hook (sometimes the weight is shaped like a fish) into the water. The hook is called a jig because the fishers must move it up and down—like it's dancing a jig—to woo the fish. The aroused fish swims close and gets hooked in the chin. Then the fisher reels up the line on two thumbs. The process is quick if you are good at it. Each fisherman would land four or five for every one I caught.

A school of cod swims close to the bottom.

This cod jig on a hand line is weighted so it drops straight to where they swim.

FISHING FOR MONEY

The only way for commercial fishers to make ends meet is to capture large numbers of fish. This is not, as some suggest, about greed and wealth—it is about earning a living. Since ancient times the goal of fishing has been to catch as many fish as possible. However, modern fishing devices have become too efficient. Every popular species of fish in North America is in danger of being destroyed because of this efficiency. Now the challenge is for fishers to earn a living while limiting the numbers of fish they catch.

Long-lining is one example of a technique that has allowed us to catch too many fish at once. It's a logical idea. If you catch a fish with a baited hook on a line, wouldn't it be an improvement to have numerous baited hooks on a much longer line? This became a productive but dangerous way to catch fish. In the early days of long-lining, large vessels would sail to fishing grounds and drop two-person rowboats known as dories. Each dory had a tub with a long

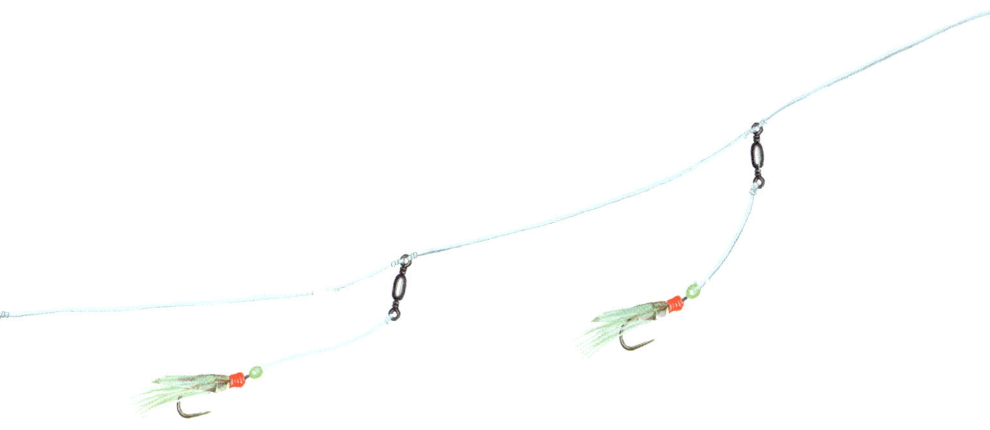

The multitude of baited hooks on a longline allows commercial fishers to catch more fish in one go than our oceans can support. The line can be miles long, and it may be a long day's work to haul in and unhook the catch.

line of baited hooks. These small boats would sometimes be overturned by a sudden wave, or become unable to find their way back to the mother ship in the fog, or catch too many fish and sink from the weight of them. Many dorymen were lost at sea.

But once ship engines were developed, long-lining changed. As people fished from larger, engine-powered vessels, they could avoid slack in the lines by hauling at a constant speed. This straightened the line and allowed them to fish many more hooks on much longer lines. The average longline is now 28 miles—and many are longer than that. It can take 24 hours to completely haul in a line.

Over time alternative commercial fishing techniques were developed, such as the purse seine, a hanging circle of

> Modern fishing devices have become too efficient, and every popular species of fish in North America is in danger of being destroyed because of this.

netting whose bottom edge is drawn together at the center, like strings closing a purse. When a school of fish swims over it, the entire school is caught.

Gillnetters put out a wall of netting and wait for fish to try to swim through it; the fish are then snagged by their gills in the squares of netting (see page 119).

Trawlers, known in New England as bottom draggers, are the most deadly of all. Sizeable ships cruise with large nets trailing behind them, scooping up everything in their path, including fish that no one wants to buy. Much is thrown away, and between long-liners and bottom draggers, many commercially unimportant but biologically important fish, such as sharks, are lost. And as the trawls drag along the bottom, they destroy habitat for bottom-feeders and shellfish.

Most commercially caught fish are not caught because of their desperate hunger. They were just swimming by and suddenly something awful happened. The fishers on a trawler cannot control how much the net scoops up. Trawled fish are probably dead by the time they land on the deck; this means that limiting the amount of fish that can be brought to market, as some environmentalists request, accomplishes nothing, nor does throwing some fish back. If a regulation says that only one thousand pounds of cod are allowed and the trawler catches two thousand pounds, one thousand pounds of dead cod are thrown away.

Most commercial fishers, if they try sportfishing, are not very good at it. It is a different way of thinking. Commercial fishing is hard physical work. It can be exciting, and it is dangerous. Even today, with satellite phones to call the Coast Guard and wet suits that provide flotation, commercial fishing is considered the most dangerous job in America.

Fishing boats are caught in sudden storms, flipped over by unpredictable waves. A fisher can get caught in an outgoing line, dragged overboard, and drowned. I find bottom draggers especially frightening vessels to work on. The net has large, heavy, wood-and-metal boards called doors that help spread it out in the water. These fly across the deck when the net is going out, and if you were to get hit by one, you'd have no chance.

Fishing for the fun of it is something completely different.

FISHING FROM A BOAT

The easiest way to catch a fish is from a boat, though the type of boat makes all the difference. The Indigenous people of New England and Atlantic Canada mastered fishing from artfully constructed canoes of bent wood and tree bark, which is not easy. On the west coasts of North and South America, canoes traditionally were made by digging out a single log. The Nimiipuu, or Nez Perce, of the Pacific Northwest fished the Snake River in dugout canoes, with spears tipped with bone or antler, and coastal peoples

throughout West Africa have long used, and still use, dugout canoes for fishing. Since at least 200 CE, Polynesians have been using outrigger canoes, which have a pontoon off of one side for stability. These are particularly seaworthy canoes, but it still takes a great deal of skill to land a large seagoing fish from one.

While canoes were originally used for net or spear fishing, modern-day sportfishers enjoy the challenge of fishing from a canoe with a rod and reel—bass fishing in the lakes of Maine or the demanding sport of canoeing for Atlantic salmon in Quebec and Maritime Canada. It requires skill to position the canoe in the current with paddles and to keep balanced while fighting a strong fish. I have fished in dugout canoes in South America and West Africa and found it to be a tremendous test of balance. Casting is not easy, but once a fish bites the line, the problems really begin.

Positioning a canoe with paddles in a current while fighting a strong fish is a real feat and test of balance.

Today most anglers cast with medium-length rods from boats with motors; these boats can be easily positioned and controlled. Anglers on boats sometimes use bait, usually chunks of herring or squid. Herring used to be one of the most plentiful fish in the Atlantic. With the seas warming from climate change, herring are vanishing while squid prosper. Squid is good bait, too.

Sometimes, especially for fish that live in fresh water instead of the ocean, fishers use artificial bait made of metal, colorful plastic, or wood.

Dragging a lure (artificial bait) off the side of a moving boat works if you have the right speed. Fish are very sensitive to speed and motion. A little added movement from the rod sometimes helps. It can be a very small movement. For some fish just gently pushing one's thumb on the rod works. Most lures are designed to move in the water with the help of the fisher, who animates the rod in jerks and dips or small vibrations.

You have to know your fish and what they respond to, which sometimes also means knowing the place where you are fishing for them. This is why hiring a local guide can make a big difference.

Local experts can tell you what colors the local fish are attracted to, a subject anglers love to argue about. Your

Knowing what the local fish are attracted to makes a big difference in selecting your lure.

winning lure might be bright blue feathers, or hot pink plastic, or disco metallic. Lures come in just about every color you can think of. Some people insist that fish don't care about color at all, that the colors are just to please the fisher. I don't think color is nearly as important as choosing between a dark lure and a light one, and that may depend on the time of day or the light on the water.

On an overcast day in murky water, if something bright suddenly darts by, the fish can't help chasing it.

A Sense of Smell

Fish smell underwater to find food. Some are better sniffers than others. Some fish have smell receptors in their noses, others farther back, close to the eyes. Lobsters smell with their antennae. Smelling is determined by olfactory genes. Fish have about 150, which is not impressive compared to humans with 500 or dogs with 1,000. But most fish are better at smelling than at seeing. Their eyes, which offer a mosaic of tiny images but no clear snapshot, are designed to detect movement. That is why jigging works. Odd movements attract their attention.

HOW A FISH FIGHTS

If you are lucky, the fish will fight you. Clarence Birdseye, the celebrated inventor of the commercial fast-freezing process, also invented a special reel that eliminates the fight. After you get a bite, you flick a switch, and—wheeeeeeee! Up the catch goes into your net. But he did not sell a single one of those reels. The fight is the most exciting and challenging part of fishing—the whole point. A sportfisher does not want it done automatically.

Once hooked, a fish will swim very hard away from you to the right or left. It is surprising how strong a fish is, even an eight-inch trout. Some fish will dive and then rise. The line in your reel is designed to go as far and fast as the fish. If you try to stop the line from unspooling, it will snap. You have to choose a line that is appropriate for the fish—not so thin that it easily breaks but not so thick that the fish does not have a fighting chance to break free. If all you wanted to do was catch a fish, you could use steel cable (usually illegal), but you want a line that offers you an exciting contest.

A smart fish will swim toward you and then quickly away. If the fish loosens the tension in the line, the line will snap when the fish pulls it back. So you have to think like a fish to win the fight. Give more line when you sense the fish needs it. Reel in the line when you sense the fish is doubling back.

The reel also has a role to play. It has a device called a drag that determines the ease with which the line leaves the reel. The fight is a contest between you and the fish for who will tire out first. If the drag is tight it will be very tiring for the fish. But if it is too tight, the fish might break your line or your rod.

If the drag is too loose, the fish can run long distances without tiring, and the angler tires out trying to reel it back in. The fish could even take all the line.

You have to let the fish run, then feel when it is tiring and start reeling it in again. In a good fish fight, the fish will go out any number of times, get reeled partly back, and run again. The hope is that slowly you will gain on the fish. When the fish is tired out, it lets you reel it all the way to where you are ready to scoop it up with a handheld net. But sometimes, right before you're about to net it, it seems to realize what is happening. Sockeye salmon often make this last stand. Seeing the net, the fish quickly darts out on one last run, taking much of the line you worked so hard to reel in.

A salmon takes a fly gently. The fisher must pull hard to secure the hook in the fish's mouth—but not so hard that the fly is yanked out.

Once the salmon realizes that it is not food, he fights the hook fiercely.

WHAT A SMART FISH KNOWS

A smart fish knows whether to get unhooked or break the line. Getting unhooked is a matter of a gymnastic tumble, a flip or a somersault. This is why the first thing the fisher must do is called "setting the hook." This is a matter of a pull or a jerk to get the hook firmly embedded in the fish's mouth. If you set too quickly or too hard, you will pull the hook out yourself. This often happens.

You have to know the fish. For bluefish, set hard the instant you feel the bite. For Atlantic salmon, wait a few seconds and then pull firmly to the side. An Irish guide once told me to say, "God save the Queen" before pulling, a most un-Irish formula. It would work as well to say, "God bless Ireland," as some Irish fishers do. Setting the hook is one of the most important battles in catching a fish.

Smart fish seem to know that the way to unhook or break the line is to create slack. Fish can do this by swimming toward the fisher, forcing them to reel madly to try to keep the tension on the line. Another nice trick for fish is to jump in the air. It is almost impossible for the fisher to keep the line taut when the fish is jumping.

Once, on Idaho's Big Wood River, I saw a rainbow trout circle a fisher several times until the man was tied at the ankles. But the fisher swooped down his landing net and caught the fish anyway. It is always a mistake for a fish to swim within range of a landing net.

This fight can take more than an hour with a good strong fish. The fish is furious, fighting for survival. A fish rarely gives up until its last ounce of strength is spent. Or perhaps not the last ounce, because the fish struggles furiously once it is landed, too, still trying to escape when the effort is clearly futile.

Salmon can leap five feet into the air to catch insects, pass over dams, or toss off a hook.

FISH FIGHTING STYLES

Some fish are better fighters than others, regardless of size. Cod and flounder are very pleasant fish to eat but not that much fun to catch. They just give up, and you can reel them in like pieces of wood. Once, fishing from shore in Gloucester, Massachusetts, one of the great codfish capitals of the world, I thought I had a cod on my line. It didn't fight or struggle, but I could feel its weight as I reeled in. It turned out to be just an old blue shirt. A cod fights as hard as a wet shirt.

The better the fighter, the more fun the fishing. Anglers will fly all over the world for a good fight with a fish. Here are some fish worth traveling for.

Bluefish

Among my favorite fighters are bluefish, sharp-toothed mad dogs of the sea that tear at everything and fight furiously. While trout may be loved for their grace and charm, a bluefish's appeal is raw fury.

Striped Bass

I have probably caught more striped bass than any other fish. They are native to the Atlantic coast of

North America. I have caught bass in Connecticut, Rhode Island, and Massachusetts.

European colonizers at first mistook these impressive fish for salmon. Like salmon, bass are anadromous, which means that they hatch and grow in fresh water and then spend their adult lives at sea. They hatch in the freshwater system of the Chesapeake Bay and in the Hudson. Then they make their way north, sometimes all the way to Canada.

The striped bass is a large and strong fish. It will not go easily to the boat and will break your line if you don't play it carefully. I have caught them in the surf, by boat, and while fly fishing. They hungrily eat both shellfish and smaller finfish such as herring, sardines, and menhaden (known in Maine as pogies, where they are used for lobster bait). Stripers can be caught with lures that are silvery and have a lot of movement. But I have caught more with live bait, a chunk of herring, or menhaden. They are, along with salmon and halibut, one of my favorite fish to eat.

With climate change striped bass have become increasingly common in the northern US, including in Maine, where they are not welcome because they swim into rivers and eat the young salmon, a population that Maine is trying to restore. They also eat a lot of lobster, which is Maine's leading industry. So Mainers are very happy to have sportfishers come and fish for stripers.

In the nineteenth century striped bass were transplanted to the West Coast, where they have prospered, too. I have caught them with bait by the pilings of the bridges in San Francisco Bay, a favorite feeding spot for stripers because of the mollusks that grow there.

Bass Confusion

The word *bass* gets confusing. Many unrelated species of freshwater, saltwater, and anadromous fish are called bass. The term comes from a Middle English word for perch, though none of them are related to perch, either.

Sea bass, not to be confused with **striped bass**, often change sex—males become female and females become male, depending on the current needs of the reproductive cycle—and are a very resourceful fish. (Far more resourceful than the **Chilean sea bass**, which is not a sea bass at all but a slow-reproducing, deep-ocean species that used to be called Patagonian toothfish until marketers gave it the more appealing moniker.) Now these deepwater Chilean sea bass are being wiped out because they cannot reproduce as rapidly as they are being fished.

Then there is the **butterfly peacock bass**, a freshwater South Florida fish that, despite its graceful name, is rather ugly. But it's a good fighter, and there have been (mostly failed) attempts to introduce it in other places for sport anglers.

The most celebrated freshwater bass are **largemouth** and **smallmouth bass**, though these two are not related to each other or to stripers. Affectionately known in the South as "bubba" or "lunkers," largemouth bass are one of the most popular freshwater fish. They are large, they fight, and they can be caught with bait, lures, or flies. They like to eat crayfish and can be caught with a furry gray, red, and blue artificial fly called a Messy Craw. It may look like a crayfish to a bass, but to me it looks like a fly with a bad hair day.

Compared to largemouth bass, smallmouth bass not only have smaller mouths but don't grow as large. But they can be better sport, more acrobatic, leaping and turning and throwing the hook. You have to set the hook well for this one. Despite this you need lighter line than for the less athletic largemouth, because the smallmouth seem to have better eyesight and will see a heavy line. Smallmouth are often caught with wooly little flies called buggers. I can't decide if they are supposed to imitate an insect or a baitfish. They move a lot in the water.

Flatfish

There are more than eight hundred species of flatfish staring up from the ocean floor all over the world. Flatfish are strange animals, lying flat on one side rather than swimming vertically. Their whole face is on that one side, including both eyes. They just stare up. Evolutionary biologists are fascinated, trying to understand why that other eye moved over. And did it happen in stages? Did the back eye travel over the top of the head, or around the bottom?

Dover sole, with its sweet white flesh, is considered the best, but unfortunately it is not found in the US. It lives in the Eastern Atlantic from Scandinavia to West Africa. Personally my favorite flatfish is the Atlantic halibut. They can be huge, often over three hundred pounds, and if you managed to land one you would have a glorious feast for quite a few people. These fish are found at sea, and while not great fighters, they require some serious hauling. They are now an endangered species rarely chased by sportfishers, though catching them was once a New England tradition. Pacific halibut are somewhat smaller but still a large fish, and they have become popular for bait fishers to catch from charter boats in Alaska. Though most of these fish are in the 20-pound range, commercial fishers catch larger ones with a longline.

But there are also smaller, fine-tasting flatfish, such as American sole and flounder. I have caught them in New England by dragging a striper plug across the bottom. Sometimes they will bite it, and sometimes the hook will catch another part of their body.

Trout

Trout is almost as meaningless a term as *bass*. Biologically, trout come from three distinct genera—two of which also include salmon. They are only native to the northern hemisphere, but anglers have transported them to the southern hemisphere for sport.

The qualities all trout share: speed, strength, grace, a fondness for insects, and fighting. And beauty. Grimly, they are at their most beautiful out of water and offer a thrilling sight when first caught.

There is the richly pastel Apache trout; the red-bellied Mexican golden trout; the brilliant, scarlet-striped golden trout; and the cutthroat trout, named for its splash of red by the gills. Then there is the rainbow. When first pulled into the daylight, this most popular trout has the visual impact of a rainbow in a clearing sky.

Pound for pound, a rainbow trout is the greatest fighting fish in the world. The fight to catch one will involve dramatic acrobatics. At times, when I am casting a seemingly empty stretch of river, one or two will start leaping in the air. They are probably grabbing insects, but it always seems that they are just laughing at me. Every now and then a trout will jump out of the water to catch your fly before it even lands. That is called getting the last laugh.

Rainbows are so loved that they have been transplanted everywhere, every state in the US, and 88 other countries besides. In the US they are only native to a few states—California, Oregon, Washington, Alaska, and Idaho. And rainbows are native to a few other places, such as Mexico and the Russian Kamchatka Peninsula.

In Vermont they share rivers with the smaller, native brook trout, the only trout native to the eastern US. Tourists fish Vermont for rainbows and are disappointed when they get native "brookies." It saddens me when people do not appreciate the natives. They are fast and wily in rivers where they have seen a lot of fly fishers. But, at the risk of yielding to popular opinion, there is nothing better than catching a rainbow trout.

Rainbows are always a good fight. Giving in to the old fishers' cliché that size matters, I remember Homeric battles with giant rainbows I caught in a river in Kamchatka, on the Pacific coast of Russia, that were as big as salmon (though not as large as the salmon I caught in the same river).

Salmon

Okay, there may be one fish more fun to catch than trout: Atlantic salmon.

When it is hooked it explodes with speed, and you want to explode with joy. But you have to use restraint, slowly pulling hard to the side to set the hook. If you set fast and hard, like you do with a trout, you will lose it. Once a salmon is hooked it pulls powerfully to one side and then sweeps across to the other, then leaps in the air and turns around.

A salmon can leap five feet in the air, which is a surprising trick for a two-foot-long animal with no legs. Atlantic salmon are found in Canada, Ireland, Scotland, Norway, and Iceland, but they are becoming dangerously rare. They can no longer be fished commercially, so only sportfishers get to taste them. Restaurants sometimes offer

Bluefish
Striped bass
Salmon
Bonefish
Trout
Flatfish

"wild Atlantic salmon," but that is probably a false offering. It is likely farmed. Even sportfishers are usually only allowed to take one, and sometimes not even that. Because these fish are rare and hard to catch, taking even one is an event locals will talk about.

In addition to the Atlantic species there are seven varieties of Pacific salmon—the Pacific offers greater diversity because there are more varieties of habitat. Chinook (or king) salmon are the largest. The second largest, sockeye, are one of my favorites for their high spirits. Then there are chum, pinks, the small but frisky coho, and cherry salmon, which are found only in Asia. But nothing compares with the Atlantic salmon, for whom all the others are named. Drawn as I am by its power, intelligence, athleticism, and stately beauty—and having caught Atlantic and five types of Pacific salmon—this may just be a personal prejudice. But it is a prejudice shared by most fishers who have experienced Atlantic salmon.

Bonefish

If you like to stalk fish—i.e., actually wade around in the water in pursuit of fish nearby—there is nothing better than bonefishing.

Bonefish are fast, strong, and smart—the three qualities I most like in a fish. They live in subtropical waters off Florida and around the Caribbean, as well as in the Pacific.

They feed by swimming into shallow saltwater pools, sometimes no more than a foot deep, sticking their nose into the bottom and sucking out small crustaceans. You might think this makes them an easy target, but nature has given them rare survival skills.

There is little point in casting unless you see a bonefish. And seeing one is a small miracle. Silver-sided with greenish backs, two or more feet long, they are difficult to spot against the white sand bottom. If they see you with their black eyes, they will disappear—fast. A darting bonefish is nearly impossible for the eye to register. They are there and then they are gone. This fish is sometimes called "the gray ghost."

Sometimes you can spot a bonefish while it is eating, its white tail fin sticking out of the water. Step carefully; while focused on food, the shy, silvery fish is also looking for signs of danger. And, unlike most fish, it will not lose all self-control when it finds food. If you use live bait with a bonefish rather than an artificial fly, it may be calm enough to nibble the bait off without ever biting the hook. While most fish just swallow their prey, bonefish, like tropical billfish species, are confident hunters who kill before they eat.

With bonefish, your fly or bait has to be cast so it lands on the sea bottom somewhere in front of the fish without the fish seeing you. This requires stealth and grace to match the bonefish's.

You also have to keep a finger on the line, ready to detect any slight vibration. Unlike most fish, which explode when hit, bonefish are nibblers who at first barely react. Then the animal takes off with alarming power, running out the line at high speed.

Sometimes it will go hundreds of feet and strip all the line off the reel. Sometimes it will swim right at you with such speed that you cannot reel up the line fast enough, and then it turns and breaks away. Sometimes a bonefish swims in rapid circles, which are difficult to control. It knows how to frustrate you. These maneuvers can tear out the hook, if the fisher does not react carefully.

Like a trout, once out of the water a bonefish stuns you with its beauty. This is how Zane Grey, the western adventure writer and great fishing chronicler, described bonefish: "He seemed all bars of dazzling silver. His tail had a blue margin and streaks of lilac. His lower (anal) fins were blazing with opal fire, and the pectoral fins were crystal white. His eye was a dead, piercing black, staring and deep."

The better the fighter,
the more fun the fishing.
Anglers will fly all over the world
for a good fight with a fish.

FACE-TO-FACE

There are different ways of picking your favorite fish. I've established that I like the fighters. Some go by looks. Cod—which swim with their mouths open and a vacant expression—have few fans. Pompano, by contrast, have sweet and gentle faces. Northern pike look serious and intelligent. Trout have the focused look you would expect from an animal that spends its life grabbing for insects. Mackerel look fierce, which they are, with their toothy sneers. Bluegill are very catchable, good-natured fish that eat smaller fish, insects, and plants; the males sometimes change colors to look like females, to avoid getting into fights. The bluegill has a cute face, as does the pumpkin-seed, a freshwater Midwesterner. Pickerel are sleek and elegant with big, sweet eyes, like the fish version of a movie star.

You are never face-to-face with a fish until it is caught. That is why aquariums are built. They let us observe fish life and look fish in the eye while they are swimming. But aquariums are not natural: The survival struggle is altered by humans feeding the fish. Some might enjoy watching fish kill and eat each other, which is what would happen in aquariums if they weren't fed by well-meaning employees. If left to fend for themselves, all the fish would be eaten by the biggest brute, who would eventually die of starvation.

I had a small freshwater fish tank that I maintained with my daughter so we could learn about fish. You can overcrowd a tank, and this one only had room for about a dozen fish. The first thing we learned is that even when you feed them, they sometimes eat each other. This would not be as noticeable in a large, well-populated, well-fed aquarium, but in our small community it was easy to observe that some friends were missing. We had flame red platy; purple, blue, and gold mollies; slim little tetras with horizontal electric blue and red stripes; black-and-white triangular angelfish; and yellow GloFish. Talia was particularly fond of a balloon molly, a fish so round it seemed to struggle to swim. We got a little red-tailed black shark that we were assured was not a carnivore. He would hide and was hard to find. Once we caught him eating a GloFish. Eventually we didn't see him anymore and assumed someone had gotten him. Fish would disappear. Talia would sadden each time we lost one. She would write little eulogies in the notebook we kept. Of the balloon molly she wrote, "I thought he would grow up to be a professor. He was smart and sturdy and funny."

The population got ever smaller . . . until they started to reproduce. Mollies are live-bearers—no eggs—and reproduce a lot. It got too crowded for everyone else. Soon it was a tank of mollies. But they reproduced with one another, and the offspring were not colorful but dark and ugly, the opposite of their parents, and even though these new fish were clearly genetic mutants—sprung from a too-small gene pool—they dominated until they were the only fish left. Then they started to die off, and eventually the tank was empty. It was an enactment of Charles Darwin's theory that species can only prosper with large populations.

THE ORIGINAL AMERICAN FISHERS

I have visited, chatted with, and fished with Indigenous people in New England, the Pacific Northwest, and Alaska, and many whom I met spoke disparagingly of sport-fishing—catching fish just for the fun of it—as opposed to fishing for something to eat or to sell. Of course many Indigenous people do fish recreationally, but the Native Alaskan fly-fishing guides I spoke with had mixed feelings about their profession. It's a job that pays well, but it's far removed from the fishing traditions they grew up with.

It is often supposed that throughout North America, before the arrival of Europeans, Native peoples only fished for subsistence, for their own dinners. This assumption was made because they maintained their fisheries with none of the destruction associated with commercial fishing. But the first commercial fishers in North America were Native Americans. In New England and in the Northwest, Indigenous people caught and traded large quantities of fish, managing their catches carefully, never taking so many that they depleted their supply. Early European explorers in New England, the Northwest, British Columbia, and Alaska recorded many accounts of Native people bringing them fish that they lacked the skill to catch themselves. In Massachusetts, the Wampanoag people trapped fish in enclosures made of wooden stakes, bringing fish to the Pilgrims who didn't know how to fish. The Wabanaki in Maine wove large fishnets from plants. In 1885 Albert Parker Niblack, reporting to the US National Museum on his study of British Columbia and Alaska, stated, "There is little in the art of fishing we can teach these Indians."

When Lewis and Clark made their famous expedition to the Pacific from 1804 to 1806, they found the Salish and the Nez Perce fishing for salmon in the Snake and Columbia Rivers and trading their catch with other groups. It was a base of their economy. The Chinook were so associated with the local salmon trade that their name is still used in the Northwest for king salmon. They mastered several techniques, including using lines with fishing hooks made of bone. Indigenous peoples in New England and the Northwest, as well as the Chippewa near the Great Lakes, used spearfishing so effectively it was banned by European Americans in many areas. And yet the Chippewa used no bait, only torches to lure the fish to the surface for spearing. The Salish killed sturgeon with double-pronged spears. Like some other tribes, the Nez Perce used nets attached to long poles. The Kwakiutl people of British Columbia were brilliant at cornering fish by building a wall of rocks during high tide, which trapped unsuspecting fish behind it when the tide went out.

On an island off the coast of Washington State, near the Canadian line, the Lummi people have an ancient and unique technique for catching salmon that dates back to before Europeans arrived. Barges are placed in the water to specifically fish incoming tides. Hung off their sides are green strips—today they are made from plastic—resembling eelgrass. Underneath is a net. Atop the barge is a 12-foot-high tower. The salmon are attracted to the fake eelgrass and so swim over the net. When the person in the tower sees that there is a large school over the net, they give a signal, the net is lifted like a purse seine, and the school has been bagged.

Native Americans in Alaska have their own version of tickling, too. I witnessed this in the Bristol Bay area on Lake Clark. There the Dena'ina people set up seasonal fishing camps with net traps to catch salmon, which they slowly smoked and dried for the winter. Many groups in the Northwest have this tradition. In 1941 James L. Earl of the Federal Writers' Project described this same tradition of smoking and drying salmon for the off season among the Tulalip Tribes of Northwest Puget Sound. A part of this

tradition was trade. The Dena'ina trade their preserved salmon for herring eggs from seagoing Tlingit.

Aside from observing their netting, I also saw young Dena'ina men wade into the water with their fingers spread like fighting bear claws. At just the right moment the fisher grabs the salmon or trout under the belly and tosses it to the bank, where it thrashes and twists like an angry patient in a straitjacket.

A Kwakiutl rock trap uses shallow rock walls that fish can easily swim over at high tide. When the tide goes out, the fish are trapped behind the wall. This is but one of many fish traps made from rocks, wood, or nets devised by Indigenous peoples before the arrival of Europeans. In Europe different trapping devices had been used for centuries, especially to catch salmon.

SURF CASTING

Many of us do not have boats. The solution, very popular on the coast of New England where I come from, is surf casting. This is more difficult than fishing from a boat because it requires greater accuracy: The angler must cast the lure just past the right spot, so that it seems to swim through the feeding grounds. You have to know where the fish are. Or make a good guess.

Surf casting started in the nineteenth century with aristocrats who formed sporting clubs by the seashore in the Northeast. They would line up with their rods along the waterfront, and their servants would spread lobster meat in the water. Lobster was inexpensive at the time and often used for bait or fertilizer. This technique of throwing food into the water to try to stir the fish into a feeding frenzy is called chumming.

Surf casting has changed. As with many forms of fishing, you are better off alone. A surf caster today uses a very long line, and having other surf casters around would inevitably lead to tangles. Even a few surf casters on one beach will try to maintain a respectful distance. I plan my surf casting not around when the fish are biting (morning or night) but for when I know I'll be alone on the beach.

A strong and flexible surf-casting rod, 12 to 14 feet long, allows you to cast—throw the line and lure—a long way. You do not necessarily have to cast a long way, but sometimes you do if the fish are feeding far out, so it is good to have that capability. Since you want to swim the lure through the area where the fish are feeding, it is good to land it beyond that spot. A splashy landing right in the feeding grounds would give you away.

The lure used in surf casting is light enough to float but has enough weight to shoot out for a long cast. It has several sets of hooks and multiple sections so that it moves a lot in the water. With skill you might cast the lure a hundred yards out from shore or farther.

Often the birds will tell you where to go. If aggressive fish, like bluefish, are chasing smaller fish to eat, the small fish will swim to the surface as they're chased. Then birds will swoop down to catch the small fish. You want your lure to land just beyond this spot. Then you reel in a little to make your lure struggle along with the small fish that are trying to escape two predators.

You have to reel in the lure at the speed that the small fish swim. Too fast does not look like a fish; too slow, and the lure will start to sink.

If you are fishing for stripers, they will be discriminating, cruising along, looking carefully for something delectable. But if they are very hungry, they will make a mistake—and then you've got a chance, as long as you play the fish well. You can lose a striper on the way in. I have. Everybody has.

Bluefish chase smaller fish, driving them to the surface where birds also feed on them, demonstrating the food web in action. The surf caster throws their lure into the mix.

From the Water: Bluefish Feeding Frenzy

If you're surf casting for bluefish, remember that they are either feeding or they are not. They don't snack between meals. They look for a large, fast school of small fish. When they start feeding they are beyond all reason, trying to grab as many as they can, as fast as they can, swallowing one, then another, chewing them up with their sharp teeth.

If you can get a lure "swimming" with the school at the right speed, a bluefish will bite. Reel it in as fast as you can and cast it out again and another will bite. They will be too busy in their feeding frenzy to notice the fate of a compatriot. You rarely catch one bluefish when surf casting. It is either nothing or a half dozen or more. This is why surf casters wander the neighborhood in the summer in their pickup trucks, trying to give away bluefish.

FISHING BUDDIES

Ernest Hemingway, in a letter to F. Scott Fitzgerald in 1925, listed his ideas of paradise. The list included which magazines he'd use as toilet paper and the nine-floor house he'd maintain for his nine-woman harem. One item of his that I would include on my own list was a trout stream that no one else is allowed to fish in.

I have never understood how fishing can be enjoyed on one of those charter boats with 20 anglers lined up and casting along the rails. Fishing is best when alone. If you are with a group of fishers, it dilutes the fantasy that you are facing down nature, matching your wit against a wild animal. I always search the beach or the river for an empty spot.

In Idaho, fly fishing is permitted in winter, and that is my favorite fishing time, while everyone else is skiing the slopes. Standing in an icy river may not sound appealing, but standing alone in an icy river with snowcapped mountains above lands it on my paradise list. The northern slopes offer little food in the winter, and the wildlife comes down in search of a meal. There is something entrancing about standing in a cold river with an elk on the slope watching you cast. Sometimes a thousand-pound moose will saunter up to check you out. Don't make him mad.

In Alaska and in Russia, I have had great brown grizzly bears come out to watch me. The bears were fishing the same salmon that I was, only they fish by sticking their faces in the river and grabbing the fish in their mouths. Watching them watch my artful cast, it's not hard to imagine them thinking I am a member of the most clueless species on Earth.

Of course if you get a salmon on your line, the bear may decide to take it. Never argue with a bear. Let her take it. The one time I do not want to be alone is when there are bears around.

The idea of the lone fisher is enshrined in literature from Yeats to Hemingway to Russell Banks. But even they will admit, as will I, that there are times—rare times—when it is enjoyable to share fishing. I have fished with my daughter since she was so little she stood up to her chest in a shallow river. These are my fondest fishing moments.

Some fishing is designed to be social. With ice fishing, for example, the more warm bodies, the merrier. Unfortunately, climate change means ever fewer places where the ice is thick enough to congregate.

There is evidence of ice fishing by Indigenous peoples dating back at least 2,000 years. The Ojibwe or Chippewa in the Midwest have long been ice fishers, as have the Mi'kmaq of Maritime Canada. Ice fishing was originally done by spearing fish through a hole cut in the ice. It has changed, with the invention of rods, reels, and lures, on tundra from Minnesota to Russia. Today huts are built and dragged out onto the ice. The floor of the hut is a series of hatches, beneath which holes are bored into the ice. Sometimes the hut is heated. Some even have beds. Some have televisions. Friends or family can spend days in the shack. But sometimes this, too, is the sport for a loner enjoying the solitude of a dark hut on a winter day.

Sometimes ice fishers use a lure that resembles a baitfish. But there is not space to swim the bait. It has to be jigged, moving the rod up and down. Other fishers use bait—small fish, insects, or even sometimes grains or bread. Some spear the fish. For this, decoys are used—carved and

Decoys attract fish to them, appearing to be company (rather than food), so that the fisher can spear them. Decoys are often fanciful carvings of fish imagined by the creator.

painted artificial fish. Decoys have no hooks but attract the fish for spearing. Carving decoys has become a popular folk art, and enthusiasts collect older decoys. It is all part of the culture in some northern places.

There are some celebrations that call for group fishing. I was once in Norway on the day the salmon fishing season began. Following an old tradition, a group of friends took folding chairs, beer, and liquor and settled into a riverbank drinking until midnight, when the season officially opened. Then we all stepped into the river and started casting—with drinking breaks throughout the night. No one caught anything, but this was not a huge disappointment. It is difficult to catch an Atlantic salmon, and fly fishing in the dark is especially challenging, even if you stay sober. The group fished together for a few days, and some fish were caught.

Fishing takes concentration, and group fishing is usually less productive. I confess that I always catch more fish alone than with my daughter. But that does not diminish the experience of fishing with her. She used to look so small wading into the river but cast with a grace she had learned from ballet. As I watched her cast, I saw confidence—she expected to catch a fish, though when she did it was often a stronger fight than she expected. I remember one large sockeye in Alaska that looked like he could pull her over and drag her downriver. But she kept her rod high, and when she finally landed it, the look of triumph on her face was what fishing is all about. When I look back on all my fishing experiences, being there for those moments are my favorite fishing memories.

GOING OUT FOR A SPIN

Probably the easiest way to catch a fish from a boat, a bank, or the shore is with spinning gear. Of course purists aren't usually looking for an easy way. But not all of us are purists. Sometimes nothing else is working and you run out of patience.

A spinner is a lure with a blade that spins, stirring up turmoil in the water and drawing fish to its hook. It works particularly well with freshwater fish such as pike, bass, and perch. Trout and salmon will also go for it, although often trout and salmon streams do not allow spinning because it is too easy.

The trick is to maintain a little slack
to keep the lure in motion
but not so much that a fish can snap
the line if it strikes.

You cast—usually with a slightly shorter, more substantial rod, but you could use a fly rod if you like—into the current so the lure rides back at you quickly. The rod tip is held close to the water. Often it works well to keep enough slack in the line that you can give it sudden jerks without causing the lure itself to jerk too suddenly. The trick is to maintain a little slack to keep the lure in motion but not so much that a fish can snap the line if it strikes.

There's an endless variety of spinners in different colors and shapes, made of plastic, wood, or metal. You get to choose, and then, of course, the fish chooses, too, so you might want to try out different spinner lures regularly to see what works.

In the days of tackle boxes, a fisher would lay out a variety of spinners in the different compartments. Today they are more likely to be bunched in the pocket of a backpack.

A largemouth bass chases a spinner lure. The blade at the end of the lure spins, stirring the water and attracting the fish.

WISE AND HUMBLE

To those of us who enjoy it, fly fishing is the ultimate form of sportfishing. The fisher must be wise and humble, and be willing to step into a river to try to understand it—to become a part of the moving water. The current presses against your legs, you feel the bottom with your feet, you see the water's surface close to your eye level. It's a bit like walking off the edge of the earth into another world.

You feel the strength of the river and the directions it is moving and the water temperature. You can even feel colder and warmer currents, which is useful because trout, especially in warmer weather, seek cool water. Instantly you start making the kind of calculations the fish are making, noticing where the current is swift and carrying food, where it is still so a fish can perch, and where the good feeding spots are. You'll notice the darker shady spots, where fish go to avoid the harsh light of midday. And you'll see why you are never certain what bugs are hatching unless you are standing in the river.

Fly fishing is based on the fact that certain fish—most famously trout and salmon, but there are others—are insectivores. They don't usually eat actual flies—a fishing industry term—but aquatic insects. These are bugs that hatch in the water or on riverbanks and often live parts of their lives in water. Fish seize these creatures from the water's surface and sometimes jump to catch them flying through the air.

A trout is an active hunter, searching for food most of the time. It finds food floating on the surface or sometimes in the upper stretches of the water. Usually it moves fast in swift currents. Sometimes the trout swims hard against the current to grab food. But this is exhausting. A better way is to find an area of still water, usually called a pool, beside a swift current and tread in this calm water waiting for food to rush by—then swim quickly into the current or up to the surface and grab it.

Fly fishing is not an easy way to catch a fish, which is the whole point. It is the most challenging way to catch a fish. No commercial fisher would use such a technique and reliably make a living or even feed a family. And yet fly fishing has been part of cultures around the world for a very long time.

In Europe and Asia, fly fishing has been around for millennia. A manuscript written about 3,500 years ago, during the Shang dynasty's rule of the Yellow River Valley, refers to an artificial fly for fishing. I have crossed the wide, rushing, gravel-bottomed Yellow River in Tibet. It is just the kind of river bottom that makes for great fishing . . . except that the water is almost opaque, literally yellow, with sediment. In any event the locals are mostly Buddhists who ban the practice of fishing.

The Romans wrote of fly fishing. In the first century CE, the Roman poet Martial referred to fly fishing in a way that suggests it was not a new idea:

Who has not seen the scarus rise,
Decoyed and killed by fraudful flies?

Fishing is a bit like walking off the edge of the earth into another world.

In the late second century CE, Claudius Aelianus described, in detail, fishing with a fly in Macedonia.

But the first thorough essay on fly fishing does not appear until 1496 in England. It is part of a larger work compiled by the Abbey of St. Albans on hunting, hawking, and other sports. The fishing part contains information on how to fashion the proper hooks, how to tie flies (including exact instructions for tying 12 flies), and how to cast. It even warns against overfishing. It is a manual on fly fishing that could still be useful today.

This treatise on fly fishing became famous in the following centuries. Early versions were not ascribed to any author, but later a woman named Juliana Berners was credited—a woman at a time when almost no one learned to read, especially women. The legend of this woman was embellished over the passing centuries. At a time when it was politically expedient to bolster the standing of clergy, it turned out that she was not just any woman, but a nun; and then when nobles sought to improve their standing, it turned out that she was not just a nun but also an aristocrat. It's not clear why the author was thought to be a woman, but it perhaps had something to do with female monarchs—the disputed nine-day reign of Lady Jane Grey; Queens Mary, Elizabeth, and Anne; and also Henry VIII's wives, some of whom he had a bad habit of executing. To promote women was a strong and volatile political statement. Berners's name is sometimes changed to Dame Juliana Barnes. No historian has been able to uncover any evidence that such a woman existed, and it remains a mystery who wrote the treatise. It may have been several people. But like the old newspaper joke says, "Don't let facts ruin a good story."

The popularity of fly fishing continued to grow in Europe and in North America. In recent years it has become too popular, some might argue. It is increasingly difficult to find a stretch on a good trout river where you can be alone, especially in summer.

Fly fishing has become so popular that some fishers are using it to catch fish that don't typically respond to flies (i.e., fish that are not insectivores). And sometimes it works! I once caught a striper on Cape Cod by tying a yellow fly to a bass surf-casting plug; the plug fished the fly, moving it artfully through the water, and the striper grabbed the little yellow morsel.

THE CASTING BALLET

There are two kinds of anglers: the hyperactive and the sleepy.

For some, fishing is about finding a comfortable shady spot, putting the hooked bait in the water, and drifting off while waiting for a fish to find you.

Ota Pavel, a Czech fishing enthusiast, wrote that he would lie down in a boat with his rods set and hooks baited, a tin can resting on each rod, and go to sleep. If he got a bite, the rattling of the can would wake him up. He wrote, "Of all the sleep a man can have, a fisherman's sleep is the sweetest. It is the greatest of luxuries—sleep and fishing."

Fly fishing, like surf casting, is for the other kind of angler. It is about casting, one cast after another after another, for hours of exercise, never tiring because you keep trying to perfect the cast.

Jack Hemingway, son of the writer, became one of the world's most devoted and admired fly fishermen. In World War II he parachuted behind enemy lines in France to work with the French underground and US intelligence. He brought a fly rod with him, was dropped from 1,400 feet, a very high jump, and landed in a rocky ravine with both his rod and his body intact. He made contact with the French underground, and whenever he could, he fished. When on the run, he made notes of promising streams with good gravel beds, pools, and banks to which he might be able to return one day.

Later, Jack was wounded and taken prisoner. The Germans told him that his arm had to be amputated or he could die from gangrene. He refused, explaining that his wounded arm was his casting arm and he would rather die than lose it. Both Jack and his arm survived to fish many more streams, and a man who later fished with him said, "Jack didn't ever want to quit. There was always one more cast to try."

There are two critical aspects of fly fishing: how the fly lands in the water and how it drifts in the current. In both instances, it has to act like a bug. Trout know their bugs . . . and their bug imitators.

A trout knows how a bug lands in the water. If there is a big splash, that cast is probably over. The fish has been alerted that something afoot is not quite as it should be.

Casting is a graceful art, and it is not surprising that dancers are often the best casters. In *A River Runs Through It*, his poetic and passionate novel about fly fishing in Montana, Norman Maclean quotes one of his father's casting lessons: "It is an art that is performed on a four-count rhythm between ten and two o'clock."

Maclean is describing a cast with a one-handed rod, which works well if there are no trees or bushes behind you (for the fly to catch on) and the wind is not blowing in your face.

If conditions are less ideal, there's always the roll cast, which avoids a backward flick of the fly (and therefore any branches behind you). And, if you have a two-handed

European rod—sometimes called a spey rod after Scotland's River Spey—you can try a double spey cast. I like the double spey cast, but it only works when the wind is blowing downriver. When the wind is blowing upriver, a roll, single spey, or C-snap, in which the rod gains force from swinging a wide circle, works better.

Maclean said he learned casting with a metronome. I sometimes listen to music in my head to get the timing right while casting. A cello suite, which I have been playing on my cello for years and never gotten quite right (perhaps because I don't practice with a metronome), works well. Bach is reliably rhythmic. Still, his cello suite is in three-four time, and since most casts have four beats, I recommend rock and roll, which is usually in four-four time. The Rolling Stones' "(I Can't Get No) Satisfaction" can lead to a perfect cast.

When I first took my daughter, Talia, fly fishing, she was young and small, but I still could not help suspecting that she was casting better than I was. She had been studying ballet for a number of years, and it had given her grace and a great sense of rhythm. Learning to cast is like learning a new choreography. You are given the moves and you are given a rhythm: On one, raise the rod straight up. On two, flip it slightly behind you, waiting for the third beat so the line straightens out behind you, then forward; and on the fourth beat, release the line that you have been holding down with a finger on your reel. The release is like pretending your hand is a gun. When you release your index finger, the gun barrel is pointing at the right spot.

Joan Wulff, a celebrated fly fisher, came from a dance background and has said, "I am convinced that the dancing

Learning to cast is like learning a new choreography. You are given the moves and you are given a rhythm . . .

lessons improved my casting because they taught me to use my whole body to back up my limited 10-year-old strength."

I wish I could go fly fishing with a ballet great like Rudolph Nureyev. That might be an unforgettable experience.

There are many fly fishing competitions. They miss the central point of fishing and reward those with the most accuracy. Sometimes the contestants are not even anglers, just people who enjoy participating in physical competitions.

Competitive fly casting, usually for distance, was invented in the United States in the 1860s, with some of the first matches held in New York and Chicago. By the 1880s, casting clubs organized national competitions, and in 1907 these clubs united under the National Association of Scientific Angling Clubs. The association then arranged competitions, not in good fishing spots but at prestigious sites like the reflecting pool in front of the Lincoln Memorial in Washington, DC. Though no fish are involved in becoming a national casting champion, the title improves your standing as a fisher. Skilled women fishers often enter because it is difficult for women to convince men that they are good fishing guides unless they are official casting champions.

In the real world, on a real river, casting a long distance does not necessarily make you a good fisher. I was once standing on a snowy bank of the Big Wood River in Idaho and I saw a rainbow in the water only six feet away. I carefully cast a fly about fifteen feet out and drifted it past the fish, and he took it. With the movement to set the hook, the fish was accidentally flipped onto the bank. I let him go. It didn't seem fair.

Sometimes it is better to stand on the bank and not in the river, especially if the water is very clear, so the fish does not see you. Cast a distance away but not too far (if you hook a fish you will have to reel it back). The fly should land softly in a spot where the natural flow of the river causes it to drift by where you hope the trout is waiting.

FAIR PLAY

Is fairness an issue in fishing? I think so. It is a sport, after all.

One time I was on the Caribbean island of Grenada for a tedious conference. Myself and a group of other journalists tired of the conference, which seemed of little news value, and hired a man with a boat. He had sonar. He could find the fish on his screen. Then he would tell us to cast exactly where he knew the fish were swimming. I could even see the fish taking my bait on the screen. All we had to do was reel them in. There was no chance of escape because he had rigged the rod with steel cable. After a while we were arguing over who had to catch the next fish. It was duller than the conference.

The central idea of fly fishing is to give the fish an even chance—maybe better than even, since the fish usually wins.

One day I was fly fishing the wide Snake River in Wyoming. In front of me rose the muscular, glaciered rock giants of the Grand Tetons, standing strong above the clouds. Each had its own personality—the Grand Teton majestic, the Nez Perce sharp and dangerous, Mount Owen sprawling, scarred, almost avuncular. And that was enough for me. Trout were just an excuse. Sometimes fishing is about nothing so much as being in a beautiful place.

I have never understood fishing on city docks, though many urbanites enjoy it.

I was studying the currents of the Snake, catching cutthroat trout. I caught one every third or fourth cast, took it off the hook, gently eased it back into the current, and cast again. I might have been doing this for an hour or for three. I wear a waterproof watch while fishing, but I always forget to look at it. Time does not exist when you are on the river. But fatigue does, and I needed a break. I waded to the bank and sat down next to my companion, a billionaire businessman, who was also taking a break.

As I sat down, he smiled at me and said, "Winning feels good, doesn't it?"

Though I would never have put it that way, I had to admit that this was what I was feeling. If you do it right, outsmarting a trout or a salmon with a little clump of feathers on a hook is no small accomplishment. The fish wins most of the time. Sometimes you win. Fly fishing is about playing fair, giving the fish as good a chance as possible. It's not about catching a lot of fish.

BEAUTIFUL BUGS

Casting and landing an artificial fly is just the prelude. It has to be done right for the main event, which is letting the fly do its work.

A fishing fly is a combination of feathers, beads, and sometimes wool or fur tied on a hook with various colors of thread wrapping it all together. The shaft of the hook has to be covered. The fly can stick up its head or wag its tail in a variety of configurations. There are rarely knots in fly tying, so it does not require unusually nimble fingers. It just takes practice. The pressure of the wrapping of thread holds things in place, sometimes aided by a spot of glue.

Aquatic insects spend part of their lives in the water and part above it, so the fly needs to either swim or float. A wet fly moves in the current below the surface where the fisher cannot see it. You don't know if it is attracting interest until you get a bite. Sometimes you can feel the bump or nibble of a fish who at the last minute rejected it. Floating flies, known as dry flies, have hackles, or stiff feather spikes, near the head to keep them infinitesimally

The dry fly floats at the surface, while the wet fly moves in the current below.

higher than the water's surface. I am probably typical in my fondness for dry flies. You can watch the whole process unfold:

With a dry fly the trout sees an insect floating on a swift current. It is not certain what kind of insect this is or even if it is dead or alive. It might be good eating. A closer look is needed. The trout swims right behind the fly, just below the surface. The trout rises, mouth open. This is food for the taking—but just before it bites, something does not seem right. Better not. The trout swims away.

The dry-fly fisher is standing not far away watching all this, cheering on the fish. "See it? Yeah, chase it. Looks good, doesn't it? Come on, grab it—aw, too bad!"

Flies can be bought, and there are many classics. Some fly patterns are centuries old. Anglers sometimes prefer to tie their own and have a particular idea based on the insect they have seen on their local river. New flies are invented all the time; many are beautiful.

In some cases they are too beautiful. After all, the fish is not looking for something beautiful to eat.

In the nineteenth century flies got so elaborate that birds like the bright green resplendent quetzal of Central America and the long-feathered, red-and-orange bird of paradise of Asian rainforests were driven to near extinction—all so anglers could have colorful, feathered flies.

People loved these feathers. Fashionable women wore them in hats. Do fish share this passion for feathers? Probably not. Humans who swear by elaborate flies are imagining fish with their own tastes and values. Nineteenth-century flies, especially British and Irish salmon flies, were magnificent works of art, colorful and extravagant in their shape, and with a great sense of balance in their complex design. Many ended up mounted in frames and decorating walls.

Another problem with all this is that we see a fly dry and from the side, whereas a fish sees it wet and from behind. So a great deal of the flair and ornament is lost on fish, even if they do share our tastes.

Today's fly tiers fashion simpler fare, but even this is often more colorful and stylish than is necessary. Many of the great fly tiers never fish. They make flies to attract the fishers. Megan Boyd, a renowned Scottish fly tier who never fished once, said, "There's no one more silly than a fisherman."

A wide variety of feather, furs, and colored thread for fly tying can be purchased in shops or online. Many of these items are expensive and unnecessary.

I once tied a fly called a McGinty, which imitates a dead bee. The body is yellow and black yarn, and it has "wings of white-tipped mallard feathers." Nowhere could I find white-tipped mallard feathers. I was contemplating this dilemma while walking on the Manhattan sidewalk near my apartment when a white pigeon feather blew across my foot. I grabbed it, and there was enough to make two McGintys. I haven't used them because I have not found myself on a river where there are bees. But I am confident that a trout would not reject them because they were made from the wrong bird. The fish, after all, will not know that I was supposed to use a mallard.

There are two kinds of flies—imitators and attractors. Imitators look like live things that live in the river. Attractors are flies that look "buggy" but do not resemble any known insect. They attract fish by their movement or color. Attractors usually have long feather tails, which move in the water. The fly literally wags its tail at the fish. Real insects seldom have tails.

An Adams, one of the most popular flies, looks like an insect should, and not a particularly colorful one. It usually has a light body, though some wrap a darker one, and it has long, stiff, brown hackles. It also has a long, thin tail. It is said to look like a mayfly, a caddis, or a midge. Of course these three flies don't look alike, and none looks exactly like an Adams. But the Adams comes closer to an insect than most attractors. Though it doesn't look exactly like any known insect, the Adams works. And some fishers succeed in catching fish with a purple Adams, which definitely does not resemble any natural insect. The Adams I tie is fluffier than most, due to my lack of tying skill, but I don't think the fish mind.

Imitators imitate all kinds of things, not only insects. There are imitator flies that look like frogs and some that look like mice. When anglers commonly smoked cigars, they discovered fish were attracted to the butts they threw in the river, and so a fly called a bomber, designed to resemble a cigar butt, was invented. There are not many cigar-smoking fly fishers these days, but the bomber is still tied, and sometimes it works. Part of the excitement of fly fishing is that anything is worth a try. It might work.

Flies often have fanciful names such as Quack Doctor, Cow Dung, Queen of the Waters, Annihilator, and Rat Faced MacDougal.

Fly fishers love their flies. I stick favorite flies in my fishing hat, some that I have tied and some great ones that others did. But the flies in a fisher's hat are like the books on the nightstand. They are the last ones you ever get to.

THE MYSTERY OF SALMON

Logically, once a salmon reenters its river on its final journey home to reproduce and die, it should not be interested in artificial flies, real flies, lures, or bait. It is not eating.

To choose a fly to catch trout, you examine what the fish in that river are eating that week. For salmon this is more difficult because they are eating nothing that week. Many times scientists and anglers have opened the belly of salmon who have been caught in a river, and there is never any food in the stomach. Yet they might bite on your fly of feathers and thread. It is the greatest of fly-fishing mysteries.

Salmon are born in rivers, but while still small they swim to sea, where they eat voraciously and grow to many times their original size. After years of far-flung feasting, the fish return home to the exact spot in the river where they were born. There they spawn and produce the next generation.

It is not known how they find this original spot. There is some evidence that they can navigate magnetic fields, which spiny lobsters and a few other marine animals can also do. Other scientists think they are guided by scent. Salmon, and most other fish, can smell food. That is the advantage of live bait over artificial lures. Once in the river they can probably smell their way, even hundreds of miles, to the place of their birth. But can they really recognize the scent of their river birthplace from thousands of miles out at sea?

The returning salmon is not like any other target for anglers. The salmon is not thinking about food, only sex. This is one of nature's ingenious designs. If the salmon unleashed the huge appetite and hunting skills developed at sea, it would eat most every creature, including all the fish in a river, killing off the trout and even new generations of young salmon. A school of such salmon could clean out a river in a matter of weeks. Mammals and bird predators would starve.

But this doesn't happen; the returning river salmon are like abstemious monks (except for the sex part). Thanks to their rich ocean diet, they have built up enough fat and protein, storing enough energy to make the arduous journey upriver against the current, leaping waterfalls, shooting rapids, and getting back to their place of birth to spawn. For us, the most succulent salmon are the ones that have just entered the river. By the time they reach the spawning

We know how to catch
a fish that is obsessed with food.
But how to catch a fasting fish
that is obsessed with sex?

place, they are lean and exhausted and haven't eaten for weeks. After spawning, they have spent all they have, and they die—except for a few Atlantic salmon that survive spawning to go to sea again and return to spawn again. Between spawning and fattening up again at sea they are known as kelts. But there are very few kelts (except for an occasional steelhead, Pacific salmon never survive spawning), and kelts are not the salmon you want to eat. They are emaciated and worn out.

We know how to catch a fish that is obsessed with food. But how to catch a fasting fish that is obsessed with sex? If the salmon are not eating real flies, why do they every now and then swallow an artificial fly? There are almost as many theories about this as there are salmon fly fishers. Some say it is because the salmon have memories of when they were juveniles in the river feeding on flies. But if that were true, why is it that they never swallow a live insect? Some say that if an artificial fly is large, colorful, and outlandish enough, the salmon will find it irritating and so snap at it. Others say that such a fly whets a salmon's curiosity. And still others say that a good fly tier can make an artificial fly irresistible—more irresistible than anything found in nature. Lee Wulff, husband of Joan, and also a renowned fly fisher, compared the salmon's urge to bite an artificial fly to the urge of a boy to cross the street just to kick a can. Scottish fly tier Megan Boyd said, "You can say what you want, but everyone is puzzled over why a salmon takes a fly."

Glenda Powell, my guide on the River Blackwater in County Cork, Ireland, who says she's always trying to shed a few pounds, remarked, "I'm not supposed to eat chocolate, but every once in a while someone will pass a chocolate in front of me, and I'll just grab it."

Whatever the reason, most fishers agree that a salmon fly should look nothing like a real insect but should be flashy and noticeable. Since there is no agreement on why salmon take flies, there is also little consensus on what attracts them. Starting in the eighteenth century, it was believed that salmon flies need to be large. Some said that salmon flies should be tied to large hooks with six wings, as opposed to the usual two wings that insects have. The belief was that the salmon, concentrating on its mission, could be distracted by this strange object, i.e., "What the hell is that?"

This idea that salmon flies need to be large endured into the twentieth century, but its logic—that a large fish wants something large to bite on—is faulty. It has since been clearly demonstrated that even the largest salmon will bite on a small fly.

Another eighteenth-century notion has proven to be more enduring: that salmon flies should be "gaudy." The notion held through the nineteenth century, when salmon flies became ever more ostentatious, particularly among the Irish, English, and Scots.

A nineteenth-century Jock Scott fly—it resembles a butterfly—was and still is one of the most popular salmon flies. They can be tied with more than 30 different materials, but the following 22 are essential.

Recipe for a Jock Scott Fly

This nineteenth-century Scottish salmon fly requires 22 essential components, including specialty feathers specifically prepared by suppliers for fly tying.

Black prewaxed thread
Fine oval silver tinsel
Yellow floss
Golden yellow floss

Feathers:
Golden pheasant crest
Golden pheasant tail
Indian crow
Black ostrich herl
Toucan
Speckled guinea fowl
White-tipped turkey tail
Peacock sword
Peacock wing
Yellow, scarlet, and blue swan
Speckled bustard
Florican bustard
Teal
Black-barred woodcock
Brown mallard
Jungle cock
Blue chatterer
Blue and yellow macaw

Today's flies are less flashy than their predecessors but are still very colorful. Like an arresting painting or photograph, an effective salmon fly has a sense of balance to its composition. Do salmon, looking up from behind, really care about that? Probably not, since you get little sense of balance from the rear view. But it is possible that a well-balanced design swims better. In any event we look from the side, taking in the pleasing balance, and buy the fly.

An Irish fisherman taught me to tie a Cascade, which is a popular and effective salmon fly, with just three or four parts. Mine has an orange feather body, a spiky red hackle, and a sparkly tail. Some tiers add wings from black squirrel fur, which is easily available from fly shops. It works.

The Jock Scott and Cascade are both popular flies for catching Atlantic salmon.

On Alaska's Copper River prized sockeye and Chinook salmon swim upstream to spawn, and anglers try to attract them with bright flies.

FISHING BY THE SEAT OF YOUR PANTS

Before the appearance of waterproof pants, fly fishers stood on shore, casting with their rods across the water. If they were smart, they hid behind a tree or bush or rock, as recommended in 1653 in Izaak Walton's famous guide to fly fishing, *The Compleat Angler*.

There are nineteenth-century engravings of this kind of fishing. The problem is, if the water is still and clear—what the British call "gin clear," which may tell us something about British fishing culture—the fish can see you. They are extremely good at picking up on the movement of casting, especially when the fisher wears bright clothing (which is not recommended). A fish does not bite when it can see an angler above.

The right pants—waterproof waders—changed everything.

Waders allow the fisher to stand waist-high in cold waters and stay dry—and even sufficiently warm, if properly dressed. In the river anglers can blend in, be a part of things, feel the urgent press of the current against their legs, the water riffling just in front, the bank behind, the sounds of the river all around. It's part of the experience. When you are standing in a river fishing, you feel as though you are participating in the river's life. You are, at least for a time, a river creature.

Before waders, there were a variety of wading accoutrements available, most aimed at keeping an angler's legs dry as long as they did not step too far into the river. Among these items were wading stockings, trouting pants, and trouting boots, none of which worked in water much deeper than mid-thigh-high. In Britain upper-class anglers had another invaluable piece of equipment, known in Scotland as the "gillie wetfoot," a guide who carried the fisher through the river on his back.

Fish are good at detecting your movement, especially if you wear bright colors—a good reason to choose gray or brown.

Then came the European discovery of rubber, long used by the South Americans, who harvested it from *Hevea brasiliensis*, a tree that grew wild in the rainforests. According to a legend, which is possibly true, Christopher Columbus introduced Europeans to rubber after seeing people in what is now Haiti playing with rubber balls. But rubber did not become commercialized until 1823, when Charles Macintosh, a Scottish chemist, used it to produce waterproof cloth, from which he made, among other things, waist-high fishing trousers held up with suspenders.

Then in 1839 Charles Goodyear discovered the vulcanization process, which led to the industrialization of rubber. Galoshes, or rubber boots worn over shoes, were first made in the 1850s, their name derived from the Latin word for the footwear worn by the Gauls. The first waterproof chest-high garment, what we today call fishing waders, also appeared in the 1850s, made by the Hodgman Rubber Company of New York.

The idea of wading into rivers to fish did not catch on immediately. Sir Humphry Davy, the father of modern chemistry and a fly fisher, said it was unhealthy. Thomas Tod Stoddart, author of the 1847 *The Angler's Companion to the Rivers and Lochs of Scotland*, complained that rubber boots did not hold up well in rivers.

Only by the end of the nineteenth century did fishing magazines start writing about a new breed of fly fishers who got *into* the river to go after fish.

In the 1930s lighter and more durable waterproof materials appeared. In 1931 DuPont developed a synthetic rubber called Duprene, today known as neoprene, which is not only lighter and stronger than natural rubber but

In the river, anglers can blend in, be a part of things, feel the urgent press of the current against their legs.

insulates against cold. It was not until the 1970s, however, that warmer, lighter, sturdier neoprene waders were manufactured, making it safer and more comfortable to wade into a wide, cold river. By the beginning of the twenty-first century, 1.4 million waders were sold in the US every year.

In recent years there has been another breakthrough: the waterproof zipper! This device takes the ordeal out of getting in and out of waders. Good waders have lots of pockets, and fishers are crazy for pockets. A pocket for a knife, for the little clipper to trim the fly, for leaders to tie on the end of the line, for a spare spool of line, a box of dry flies, a box of wet flies, a camera or cell phone, a sandwich . . .

THE BIGGER THE FISH

Fishers usually want fish to be as big as possible. I am very happy with any rainbow trout, but to be honest, I would like the largest rainbow trout I can find.

The reason tourists in Vermont prefer the transplanted rainbows to the native brook trout is that rainbows are bigger. Of the seven species of Pacific salmon, kings, otherwise known as Chinook, are preferred because they are the largest, even though the slightly smaller sockeye could be a better fight, and maybe a smarter fish.

The rich will travel the world for the biggest fish. Fishers with enough money will travel to Siberia to catch taimen, a relative of salmon that grows to six feet and 60 pounds. They'll fly to the tip of South America to fish for transplanted nonnative trout and salmon that grow to enormous size.

Not everyone prefers the biggest fish. Once the author Ernest Hemingway could afford a large cabin cruiser (which he had designed to be only a few feet short of the yacht classification so it could not be said that he was yachting), he started fishing giant billfish—blue marlin and sailfish. Then he lost interest in the art of fly fishing for smaller fish.

He would take his son Jack along after the big game. But Jack never developed Papa's passion for the giant fish. He wanted to fly fish for trout and salmon. While fighting a rainbow trout cannot compare to the physical stress of fighting a thousand-pound marlin, emotionally and intellectually it can equal the excitement.

This is the finesse-versus-size tension within fishing—two different views of the ultimate fishing experience.

Blue Marlin

Blue marlin, were it not for humans, could live happy lives. They have few predators other than killer whales and great white sharks, and they spend their days out at sea, swimming near the surface, stabbing and stunning other fish, even some large ones, with their long, pointed bills and then circling back to eat their victims. In my brief encounter with marlin off the coast of Port Antonio, in Jamaica, I could see that a marlin does the same thing smaller fish do when on the hook—the runs, the leaps—it is only the scale that is different. And the sounding: A marlin can dive hundreds of feet to escape a fisher.

Males are about 300 pounds, but females are much larger. There are claims of marlins weighing more than 1,600 pounds, though none over 1,400 have ever been verified. You are sitting at the stern of the boat strapped in a chair so the fish can't pull you into the sea. That pull on your arm, the same muscles you recall from all the other fish, is now more than exciting, maybe a little frightening, like no longer boxing with amateurs. Maybe I shouldn't have stepped into the ring with this one. You are committed and may have to fight this marlin for hours. It leaps and it sounds, diving to the depth of the sea. The sight of a thousand-pound fish leaping into the air while you try to hold it with your rod straight up is one of the reasons fishers will go to great lengths to get a marlin on their line. Then there is the work of an hour or more of backbreaking struggle to land the giant. But then you have done it—conquered a giant.

THE PERFECT ROD

When the fish strikes, you lift the rod as close to straight up as possible. If the rod is held out parallel with the water, you have very little leverage. The fish pulls directly on the line, the reel, and you. By raising the rod, you gain leverage and control—the rod joins the fight.

A good rod is not stiff. It bends the way a tall tree survives a strong wind. While the bottom part stays straight up, the fish pulls down on the tip so it becomes almost U-shaped. The rod helps fight the fish. But the rod can lose. The fish can double the tip over until it snaps. A good rod bends but does not easily break.

Each rod is forged for its unique purpose: long rods for surf casting, short rods for ice fishing, light rods for trout, sturdy rods for marlin. The more unique the casting challenge, the more thought goes into the rod making.

How long and how flexible is a good fly rod? The whip of the rod, its ability to bend, is part of the cast. You want the rod to work with you.

According to ancient Roman accounts, some used six-foot rods. In later centuries, European writers describe them as twice or even three times that length. As better materials were found, longer rods were built.

British officers in India started bringing bamboo lances back to England as souvenirs in the 1700s. Some were used as fishing rods, while others, broken into smaller pieces, became favored as rod tips. However, regular knots in the bamboo kept it from being a clean rod, so rod makers started cutting the bamboo into strips with beveled edges and gluing them together with no knots.

Six strips of bamboo, triangularly shaped to fit together, glued and wrapped with silk thread, produced a tapered hexagonal rod. It was demanding and time-consuming to plane the triangular strips in so they fit together, but when done well this produced the best fly rod anyone had seen. It was lighter, stronger, and more flexible than any rod in history.

The demands of rod making, and the ever-present possibility of making a better rod than has ever been made before, cause some rod makers to become even more obsessed than fly tiers. Fishers thus afflicted often abandon fly tying for rod making. One of the early split-cane rod makers, Thaddeus Norris, said in his 1864 *The American Angler's Book*, "Anglers are apt to become fastidious as to the spring and taper of their rods, especially those used for fly fishing."

Some rod makers use more than six strips. The more strips, the more difficult the work of rod building, but the rod can have better action and flexibility. A number of rod makers in North America, Europe, and Japan make eight- and even nine-strip rods.

Bamboo's combination of light weight, strength, and flexibility make it an ideal substance for fishing rods. Also, unlike many other rod materials, cane does not continue to vibrate after a cast is completed, making it less tiring to use.

In 1947 fiberglass rods came into use. They were solid at first, but by the 1950s hollow fiberglass rods had become very popular. Fiberglass rods are made of thin glass fibers molded into tapering shells and are extremely elastic, perhaps as elastic as split bamboo, and far easier to make and much cheaper to buy.

While working on advanced aircraft design in the late 1960s, the Royal Aircraft Establishment at Farnborough in South London made a stronger material called carbon fiber. No one will give any details of how exactly that came about, but I like to think that some aerospace engineer who was also a passionate fly fisher discovered the new material and instantly realized that it would make a great fly fishing rod. In any event, it does.

Carbon rods, which range in price, are considered the best rods for the money today. But new ideas for rods are always being tried out. A $2,000 titanium rod and rods made of boron are among the newest ideas, but more will be coming. Two thousand dollars may be a lot for a rod, but good split-cane rods start at that price, too.

Then there is always something "new" being resurrected from the past. The Japanese tenkara fishing rod is making a comeback. The tenkara rod was developed in the twelfth century, possibly as part of the training of a samurai warrior. The rod seems to have the Zen elements of patience, contemplation, and simplicity, perhaps because, like a fifteenth-century European rod, it has no reel. The line is simply tied to the end of the rod. Unlike the old European rods, though, the tenkara is lightweight, and its line is longer than the rod (an old European formula said the line should match the length of the rod).

The tenkara appeals to purists, the dry-fly type. It is held high so that little of its line goes in the water, forming a direct line from fish to rod tip, with less line in the water to scare away a fish. When a fish bites, the rod is held even higher and back a bit so that the fisher can reach up, grab the line, and pull in the fish with his hands. This feels like the basic fishing of my childhood.

Originally, tenkara rods were made of bamboo, but they are now made of carbon fiber. They have no line rings and can telescope down into very small sizes that are easily packable in suitcases—the most portable tackle imaginable. Once I was fishing with a tenkara in a national park on an afternoon when I had accidentally let my fishing license expire by one day. A ranger passed by but did not recognize my tenkara as a real fishing rod and so did not fine me.

I once had a great time catching frisky little cutthroats in the Snake River with a tenkara, but I can't imagine using it to catch a salmon or a big, hard-fighting rainbow, because it has no line to run out. Your rod has to be well matched to the fish you are pursuing.

I own seven rods—an old 14-foot surf-casting rod, two shorter boat rods, and four fly rods, including a tenkara and a two-handed spey rod from Scotland. I do not use a split cane or a titanium rod, because you can love a rod too much. When you are struggling to hold up your rod, fighting a fish that is bending over the tip, you do not want to have the thought that if the fish breaks the tip, you are out thousands of dollars.

But Thaddeus Norris understated it. Anglers are more than fastidious about their rods. I enjoy taking them out of the closet to choose one for an upcoming trip. I love my rods.

WOMEN WHO FISH

Women have fished for a long time—since long before the myth of Dame Juliana—disproving the always-dubious belief that fishing is all about testosterone and proving your masculinity.

It is said that Cleopatra fished in ancient Egypt, which probably burnished her reputation as a woman of intrigue.

Seventeenth-century English poet Edmund Waller in Elizabethan England wrote about fly-fishing women:

At once victorious with their lines and eyes,
They make the fishes and the men their prize.

It was acceptable for women to fish in seventeenth-century England (well, at the time the country was also run by a woman), but until the twentieth century there was no suitable women's clothing for fishing. Casting and fighting fish from a bank trussed up in a floor-length dress seems heroic. Nor was tackle made for the size of women—rods were heavy. Even the heavy tackle suggested in Dame Juliana's *Treatise* was unsuitable for the average woman.

Women have historically been a rarity on commercial fishing vessels, although today they are making some inroads. There are women lobstermen in Maine, and they generally refuse to be called lobsterwomen. There are some women gillnetters in Alaska. Indigenous people often saw certain kinds of fishing as women's work and certain kinds as for men. Among the Chipppewa ice fishing and spear fishing were only for men, but netting was only for women.

There are two centuries-old myths about women and fishing that still persist. One claims that women bring bad luck. When I worked as a commercial fisher in the 1960s, there were still fishermen who were horrified when a woman stepped on deck. The bad-luck myth seems to be losing favor, but many men still believe the other myth—that fish *like* women, and that it will be a better fishing day if there are women on the water.

Some of the earliest records of women fly fishing are nineteenth-century Norwegian descriptions of British aristocrats who set up fishing camps along their salmon rivers. In 1863 Percival Hambro and Augustus Stewart fished the Stjørdalselva with their wives, who were possibly the first women to fly fish a Norwegian river. The well-dressed ladies stood on the birch- and alder-covered slopes of the banks, casting into glassy pools by the rapids and falls of the rushing river, catching trophy salmon. It appeared they'd done considerable fly fishing in England before this particular trip to Norway.

The founder of Pennsylvania, William Penn, raised a daughter, Margaret, to fish. Around 1737 she wrote to her brother in England saying that fishing was her "chief amusement" and asking if he could buy her "a four jointed strong fishing rod and reel and strong good line and assortment of hooks, the best sort."

The state of Oregon started requiring men to purchase fishing licenses in 1899, but women were not required to have them until 1923, the presumption being that fisherwomen were not so numerous as to be a factor in fishery management. Some US states did not require women to get fishing licenses until the 1960s.

Until recent times there were also virtually no fishing clubs for women. Andrew Burnaby, in his 1798 edition of *Travels Through North America,* described a society known as the Fishing Club, composed of 16 women who met twice a month at the Schuylkill Club, located in southeastern Pennsylvania. The Schuylkill Club had been founded in 1732 as the first fishing club in the 13 colonies. The first bona fide fishing club for women, the Woman Flyfishers Club, was founded in New York in 1932.

One of the great British fly-fishing legends is Georgina Ballantine. On October 7, 1922, she was fishing the River Tay in Scotland on a boat handled by her father, who was the fishing official on the Glendelvine Estate through which the river runs. She was having a respectable day catching good-size salmon. She was fishing two rods—one with a Wilkinson fly, a salmon fly with a long, feathery tail, and the other with bait. A salmon grabbed the bait and she fought it for most of an hour, trying to get it to the bank. The fish was so large and so strong that even when she finally got it to the bank, she could barely lift it. According to one account, she sat on it. It weighed 64 pounds and was four feet six inches long. That is the standing record for the largest rod-caught salmon in Britain.

But since Ballantine caught the salmon with bait, the record for catching the largest salmon with a fly was still open to challenge. Two years later another woman, Clementina Morison, popularly known as "Tiny" Morison, caught a 61-pound salmon from a highland bank of the River Deveron with a fly known as the Brown Wing Killer.

Records aside, for decades Mary Orvis Marbury, born in 1856, was the world's leading fly expert. Even today there are few people with the depth of knowledge she had. She grew up during the years when her father, Charles Orvis, was just starting to establish his famous fly-fishing shop in Manchester, Vermont. He hired experts to teach his daughter how to tie flies, and at the age of 20 she became head of the company's fly division. Working with her in an upstairs workshop were six other women fly tiers.

Other women set up other fly-tying shops staffed with women tiers. In 1890 Carrie Frost started a fly-tying shop in Stevens Point, Wisconsin, and 60 years later the town was known as America's leading fly-tying center, the shop still staffed mostly by women.

People in the sportfishing industry like to say that women are the fastest-growing demographic group in fly fishing, but in fact they are the *only* demographic group that is showing significant growth.

Cornelia Crosby, six feet tall, often referred to as Cornelia "Fly Rod" Crosby, is a nineteenth-century Maine legend whose skill with a fly rod was only one of her outdoor talents. As a hunter she was reputedly a great shot and is rumored to have gone shooting with Annie Oakley. Born in 1854 in Phillips, Maine, a railroad center on the Sandy River in the interior of the state, she is said to have honed her fly-fishing skills as a teenager with the help of local guides. She earned a reputation for the many large salmon and trout that she landed with her bamboo rod. One day in 1886 she landed two hundred trout. She was also known as a highly skilled fly-tier. She became a national fishing celebrity, in part because of her nationally syndicated column, "Fly Rod's Notebook," which was often about girl and women fly fishers. She once wrote, "I would rather fish any day than go to heaven."

Railroads hired her to give talks on fly-fishing destinations. She advocated for more suitable clothing for women anglers and created a sensation with a fishing skirt that only went down to the knees.

In the 1920s, when Maine was a leading fly-fishing destination, one of its celebrated anglers was Carrie Stevens. In 1924, at the age of 42, she tied her own fly for the first time. She used gray feathers, designed the fly to resemble a minnow, and landed an enormous 13-pound brook trout—a monster brook trout. Stevens called her fly the Gray Ghost, and once word of her monster got out, she could not tie enough of them to keep up with demand. She produced about two thousand flies a year and sold them for $1.50 each, which in today's dollars would be an annual income of $55,000. A fly-tier has to tie a lot of flies to earn a good living.

In the twentieth century companies began to develop tackle more suitable for women, starting with lightweight one-handed rods and lightweight reels. But waders still presented a problem. Standing in a strong current in large, heavy, awkward waders can be dangerous. The fisher can be swept away.

Waders of sizes and a fit more suitable for women started to be introduced in the mid-1970s.

Today about 6.5 million Americans fly fish. A third of them are women, and that percentage is growing. People in the sportfishing industry like to say that women are the fastest-growing demographic group in fly fishing, but in fact they are the *only* demographic group that is showing significant growth. The leading outfitters, including Orvis, have launched education and training programs to bring more women into the sport. Soon fly fishing will no longer be a male bastion.

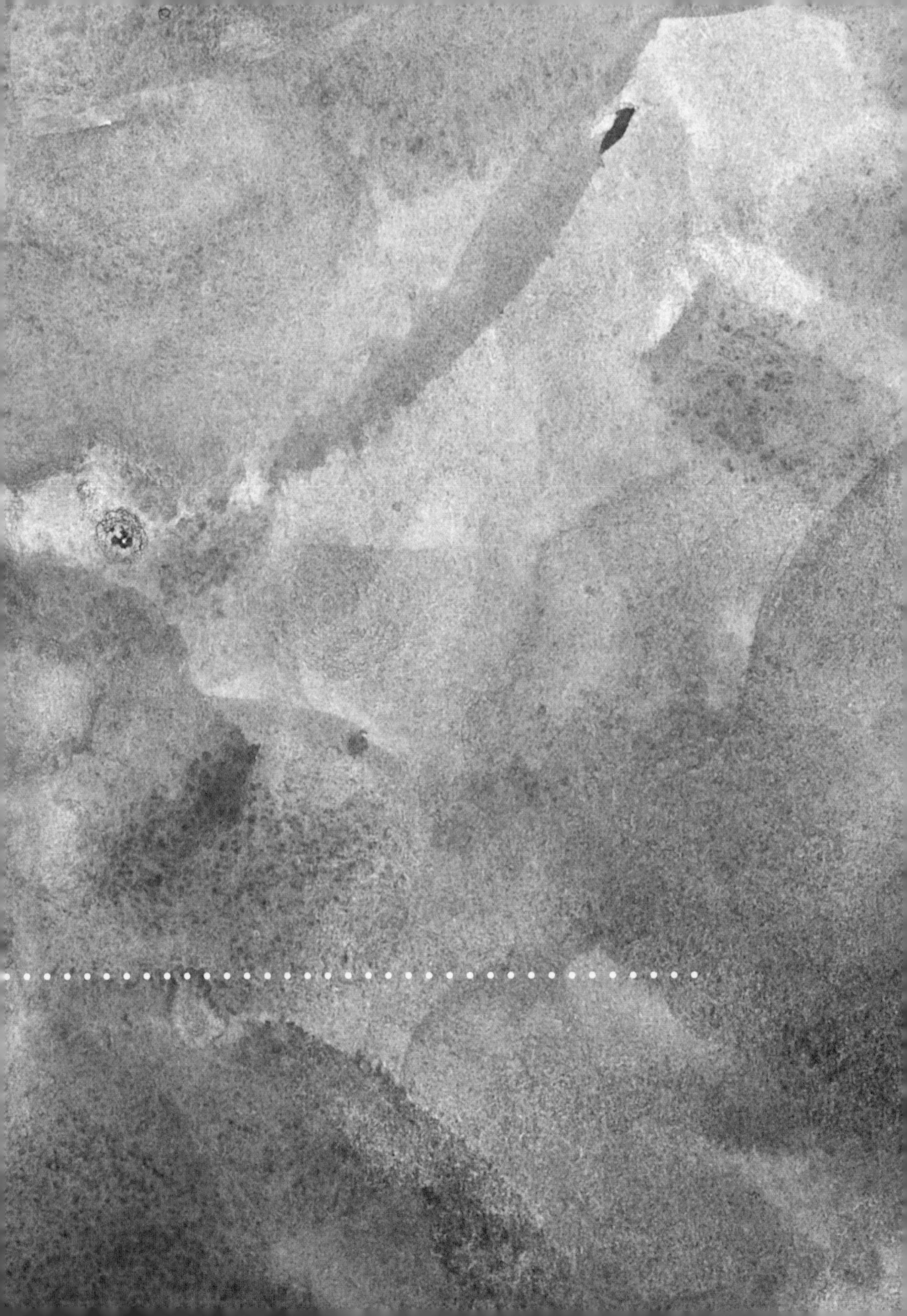

PART TWO

WHAT DO I DO WITH IT NOW?

KEEPERS

The first question the fisher asks after the triumph of landing a fish is, do I want to keep it? On a good fishing day you catch more fish than you want. Often you want just one and throw the rest back. On some rivers it is illegal to keep fish, or sometimes just one is allowed. Throwing fish back alive is often called "catch-and-release."

Some people have a low opinion of catch-and-release fishing. Isn't it an insult to nature to catch more fish than you want to eat or sell? Isn't hooking a fish just for the fun of it cruel?

Some fish are becoming so scarce, such as Atlantic salmon, that keeping them is very restricted. The key is to throw them back without harming them. After all, you have already put the fish through considerable trauma. You cannot land a fish until it is exhausted. Some critics say released fish do not survive. Though this may sometimes be true, it clearly is not in most cases. Any regular angler can testify that many lively fish they catch bear signs of having been caught before. Fish do learn, and it is true that fish are more difficult to catch in a thoroughly fished river.

Sometimes, despite best intentions, the "release" doesn't work out. Fishing cod in a skiff off Newfoundland, catching, tagging, and releasing for the Canadian government, we were all inexperienced with the tool that shot the tag into the fish. Sometimes we had to try several times before a tag stuck in, and by then the fish was dead. On the plus side, there is nothing better than a freshly killed cod cooked in sea water.

Another time, in Alaska, when my daughter was very small, she caught a very large sockeye salmon. We were going to throw it back because I had already caught one.

But we had to get a picture of little Talia and her giant salmon. The fish was too big and strong, and she kept dropping it. By the time we got the picture the salmon was dead. I'm still sorry. It was also delicious.

If you want to throw the fish back, you are better off leaving it in the landing net in the water until you unhook and release it. But then there are those pictures. They are a kinder substitute from earlier centuries when the fish was stuffed and mounted. But they result in suffocated fish. If you insist on snapping the photo with the fish out of water, try to rest the fish's body on a flat hand while holding the tail just before the fin with a thumb and index finger. Warning: Fish are strong and slippery, so it doesn't always work out.

Also it is sometimes difficult to remove a well-set hook without injuring the fish. Some fish are easier to release than others, and even the most careful fishers will sometimes destroy a fish that they are trying to release. Bluefish are a good candidate for catch-and-release because you often catch more than you want. But they are vicious animals with sharp teeth, and they will bite your fingers, even when you're trying to set them free. Some people use pliers to remove a hook; this is difficult to do without harming the fish, even if it does save your fingers.

One solution is the barbless hook. The barb is a sharp point on a hook that goes in the opposite direction of the hook's main point. A barb holds the hook in a fish's mouth. Without a barb it is much easier to slip the fish off, but it is also much easier for the fish to slip itself off before you catch it.

But sportfishing is about creating challenges, not about making it easy.

Throwing a fish back without harming it is a challenge, and the fish doesn't always survive.

Catch-and-release was never really about being nice to fish. It was environmental, about preserving fish stocks. Lee Wulff, a famous fly fisher and an early promoter of catch-and-release, said, "A good game fish is too valuable to be caught only once."

But often in areas that are well fished, fish will show signs of having been caught before.

IS IT CRUEL TO CATCH A FISH?

Many have wondered if fishing is cruel to the fish. It is difficult to fish and not think about this. Is being dragged by a hook in the mouth not painful? At first glance the answer seems obvious. Of course, how could it not be? If someone put a hook in our mouth and dragged us, this would surely hurt a great deal. But fish are not people. They do have some nerve endings, but not many, and only a few are in the mouth. But whether the sensation is perceived as pain in the human sense is not clear. The most scientific answer is "I am not able to say."

The debate over whether fish that are caught and released live or die—some of each, no doubt—misses the main point. Before they are landed, unhooked, and released, they have already been put through a terrible, stressful experience. This is why some say it is wrong to catch a fish if someone isn't going to eat it. Others justify fishing with the argument that a human is a predator mammal, and that part of the appeal of fishing is acting out our natural role as a predator in nature. But is it natural to do it just for fun and then let the prey go?

When I am working a hard-fighting fish, I admire the fish's determination to fight and survive. But what if the fish is just terrified?

Catching a fish seems a natural act. A fish would understand it. But a fish would not understand catch-and-release or any hesitancy to kill.

To make fishing more challenging by trying to treat a smaller animal fairly is not natural. Animals in nature kill in the most efficient way possible. In this sense commercial fishing is more natural than sportfishing. The big grizzly bear studying me from the opposite bank doesn't get it. After all, what is the point of being large if it isn't an advantage?

But just because fairness isn't a natural concept doesn't mean that it isn't a good idea. The biologist Edward Osborne Wilson used to talk about what he called "the natural fallacy," the belief that because something follows nature that necessarily makes it a good idea. To participate in nature without causing imbalance, we sometimes have to rig things a little bit. But no matter how you approach fishing, you are still a predator.

President Jimmy Carter, a lifelong fisher who used to slip away from the White House to secretly go fly fishing with his wife, said that to fish you had to be at peace with the idea of being a predator. He advised that if you couldn't do that, you shouldn't fish.

BLEEDING A FISH

If you are planning to eat the fish you catch, the first thing you should do is bleed it. Fish anatomy makes this easy. On each side there is an aorta accessible through the gills. You can reach in with a finger, grab it, and yank it so it breaks. You have to do this when you first catch the fish so its heart can pump the blood out. This makes a huge difference in the quality of dark, oily fish such as bluefish, mackerel, or tuna. But it also improves the quality of more delicate fish flesh such as flounder or snapper.

I once fished in the Copper River salmon fishery in Alaska, one of the highest-priced, highest-quality fisheries in the world. They tore the gills immediately when they pulled the salmon from the gill net. If you want a good fish, as soon as you catch it, reach in and yank.

When I mention this to nonfishers they are often appalled. How cruel to reach in and yank the aorta of a living animal. Though the motivation for bleeding is gastronomic, it is actually one of the kinder ways of killing a fish. It is quicker than letting it just lie there and slowly suffocate. Some fishers who don't know about bleeding have a club handy to smash the fish in the head to swiftly end its suffering. Bleeding is slightly less violent, almost as fast, and probably less traumatic. Probably. Who knows?

THE SCALE OF THE TASK

There are few inedible parts of a fish. Even bones of some fish can be rendered edible if treated right. In traditional Hawaiian cooking there is a dish made from the bones of mackerel scad, known in Hawaii as opelu. (This is a small fish, easy to catch, often used as bait, and found in both the Atlantic and the Pacific.) After the opelu have been boned for other dishes, their spines are fried in coconut oil with garlic and eaten as a crunchy snack.

But there is no hope for scales. They are tough, indigestible little pieces of armor that will ruin your meal.

With the edge of a knife or a tool specially designed for the task, scrape all the scales off the fish. This is as fundamental as removing the hide from animals before cooking, though it's a lot easier.

The skin, on the other hand, once scaled, is a treat, though it of course depends on the fish. Scales protect delicate skin. Fish without scales have tough skin. Swordfish do not have to be scaled, but you wouldn't want to eat the skin, anyway. I think shark skin, which does have scales, is inedible even scaled, but it's a delicacy in Japan, as is salmon skin, which is one of the ocean's great treats. In sushi bars it is served grilled and wrapped in seaweed.

KEEPING A HEAD IN THE GAME

To me there is no more depressing sight on a dinner plate than a decapitated fish. I suppose there are people who don't like the head or, at least, that is the assumption of many restaurants. So there it lies, headless, the Marie Antoinette of ichthyology. Not only is this a reminder of the fish's violent demise and a mangling of its beautiful form, but it means you are discarding the best part of the fish.

The flesh on the top of the head, the cheeks on the side, and the throat on the bottom are the most tender, delicate, sweetest parts of the fish. The larger the fish, the more obvious this becomes. Trout cheeks are a quick little treat, barely a bite. In places with a strong cod tradition—along the Atlantic seaboard—cod cheeks and tongues are a traditional dish. The cheeks are the size of scallops, and the so-called "tongue" is actually the throat of the fish, the part under the chin.

Ukha is a popular dish in Russia. The whole fish is cooked in a stock with vegetables. The honored guest is served the head.

Salmon heads are a special treat of the Indigenous people of the Pacific Northwest. Sometimes they are cooked in a soup. Sometimes they are aged until fermented, which to my uneducated nose and palate seems rotten. The Eyak in Alaska, a nation with few members left, used to make a soup from salmon eyes, though I have to admit declining this offer. The Dena'ina people, in their fish camp in Bristol Bay, Alaska, save heads as a special treat. They cut the heads off, split them in two, and pack them with alternating layers of salt. June Balluta Tracey has 12 siblings and stays with much of her family in the Dena'ina fishing camp every summer putting up salmon. She says, "In the middle of winter we are hungry for fish heads. Take one out, soak it for three days, and make fish head chowder—the eyes and the cheeks, and suck the bones. The nose is the best."

Her recipe for fish head chowder begins, "Put the head in the water until it gets fuzzy."

The heads are soaked in the river for days, in a cage or tied to a line. I asked what she meant by fuzzy. She giggled and whispered, "A little bit rotten."

I am happy with a simple poached or baked head, but recipes can get much more elaborate. Eighteenth-century English food writer Hannah Glasse, who reported on the food trends of her time, documented a number of recipes for boiled, baked, and roasted fish heads. Here is my favorite from 1747.

To Roast a Cod's Head

Wash it very clean, and score it with a Knife, strew a little Salt on it, and lay it on a Stew-pan before the Fire, with something behind it, that the Fire may roast it. All the Water that comes from it the first Half Hour, throw away; then throw on it a little Nutmeg, Cloves, and Mace beat fine, and Salt; flour it and baste it with Butter. When that has lain some Time, turn and season it, and baste the other Side the same; turn it often, then baste it with Butter and Crumbs of Bread. If it is a large Head, it will take four or five Hours baking; have ready some melted Butter with an Anchovy, some of the Liver of the Fish boiled and bruised fine, mix it well with the Butter, and two Yolks of Eggs beat fine, and mixed with the Butter, then strain them through a Sieve, and put them into the Sauce-pan again, with a few Shrimps, or pickled Cockles, two Spoonfuls of Red Wine, and the Juice of a Lemon. Pour it into the Pan the Head was roasted in, and stir it all together, pour it into the Sauce-pan, keep it stirring, and let it boil; pour it in a Bason. Garnish the Head with fry'd Fish, Lemon and scraped Horse-raddish. If you have a large Tin Oven it will do better.

Ahh, the recipe without end—it does require considerable patience. Surprise your guests.

I once was invited to a dinner for French journalists in Dakar, Senegal, that featured a fish head. Our host, an expansive and charming government official, announced we would be eating a "capitaine." This is often the name given to the largest, most prized species in French-speaking countries, in this case a five-foot freshwater fish known as a Nile perch. The journalists appreciated the local specialty, which was large enough for all of us.

Because I had gotten into a conversation with the host about the joys of fish heads, he and I were the exclusive recipients of the head of the capitaine. It was full of delectable meats, and we pulled it apart and enjoyed one of the best fish dinners I have ever experienced.

Never try to relive the past. Years later I was pushed into a similar head conversation with a host in Amman, Jordan. This turned out to be not the head of a fish but a sheep, and what could I do once the sheep head was set in front of me on a platter? For me this was not a good experience. Fish heads are something special.

SHOWING SOME GUTS

Now that you have a fine whole fish, head and all, and it has been bled and scaled, the next step is to remove the guts. The organs of fish are in the forward part of the body, mostly under the rib cage. With a sharp knife, make a cut along the bottom of the fish, from about halfway back to the front. The fish is now open. This is not fine surgery. Just stick your hand in and yank everything out. Most people just throw this stuff away.

But wait a minute. If a seal could think in human terms, it would think you foolish. But being judgmental is probably a distinctly human trait. Marine mammals seem a lot smarter than humans about food—or at least seem to know where the high food value in a fish is found. Orcas, sometimes called killer whales, hunt the feared great white sharks, kill them, and eat just the liver, throwing the rest away. Seals usually only eat salmon guts and throw the rest out, which infuriates fishers.

Once working on a gillnetter off the coast of Alaska, we set the net, and in the morning it was full of salmon—kings and sockeyes and a few pinks. We were about to haul in the net when four seals swam over and systematically bit the bellies out of each salmon, leaving the ruined bodies hanging from the net. There was nothing we could do but stand there and helplessly watch. Seals are a federally protected species. In any event it is illegal to carry a firearm on

Suppose you could interview a seal. What would they say about the wastefulness of humans who just eat the meat and throw out all the good parts?

a commercial boat in Alaska—a good law because, on seeing the wastefulness of these gutted fish hanging from the net, you'd be confronted with an almost irresistible urge to shoot the seals, especially if no one were looking. But suppose you could interview a seal. What would they say about the wastefulness of humans who just eat the meat and throw out all the good parts?

The Roe, a.k.a. Eggs

All female fish have eggs, though none are so prized as sturgeon eggs, known as caviar. Salmon roe is excellent. If you catch a salmon, hope for a female. Alaskan salmon processors used to throw the salmon eggs out until, in the twentieth century, Japanese buyers started offering good money for them. But Native Americans always valued them. In the Northwest there is a long tradition of eating fish eggs. The Tlingit eat herring eggs; others, like the Athabaskan groups in Alaska and British Columbia, are salmon egg eaters. On the Pacific coast of Russia, where salmon is an important commercial catch, the stores sell salmon eggs in buckets.

Each bucket holds a different species of salmon eggs, and locals have strong opinions about which they prefer. The eggs are so valuable that poachers just rip salmon open for their eggs and throw the rest out. Seals would understand, but the government does not.

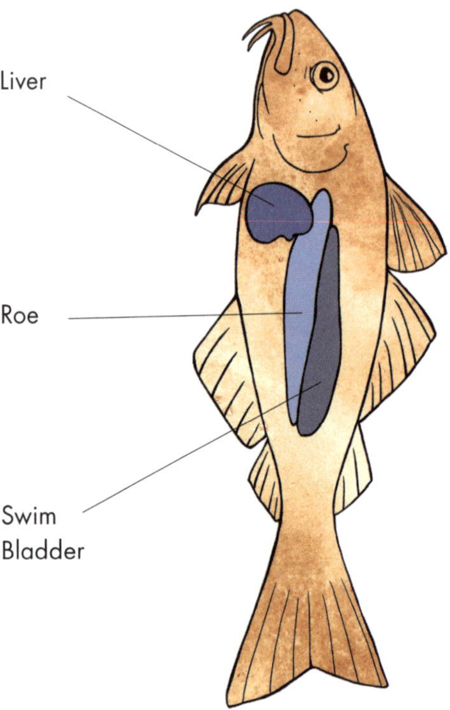

There are treasures to be found inside a fish. The valuable organs are in more or less the same places in most species, though the color may vary. The roe is often colorful (though sometimes black), the swim bladder is light-colored, and the liver usually tawny.

Italians prize smoked swordfish and tuna eggs. Fish roe in the cod and mullet families are valued in North America and northern Europe. The entire roe of pollock is eaten like a sausage. Other eggs are less appealing but are always worth a try. Even lobster roe is excellent. The ancient Chinese said that eating fish roe gave you the glow of good health. It may. It also tastes really good.

The Livers

Most ocean animals, even lobsters, have tasty livers, just like land animals. For centuries cod liver has been famous for its health-giving properties. These livers have traditionally been known for their truly awful taste, but that is only because commercial fishers saved them on their voyage in an unrefrigerated bucket. A good liver has to be eaten as soon after catch as possible. In Iceland, an old recipe called for stuffing cod stomach with the liver, mixed with grain, then boiling it like a dumpling.

But approach with caution. Livers process impurities, and if a fish lives in polluted water, the pollutants will be in the liver, and very concentrated. So only eat liver from fish caught in clean water. There are New Yorkers who like to catch and eat fish from the East River and New York Harbor. New York has been greatly cleaned up, thanks to the Clean Water Act, but I would not eat a liver from a New York City fish.

Some 40 years ago I was interviewing the great Paris chef Alain Senderens, and he invited me to lunch. He served rouget barbet, a Mediterranean red mullet, as grilled filets surrounded by toast rounds spread with the fish's liver and bejeweled with flash-fried, bright green celery leaves. The impact of both the sight and the taste was such that I still remember it. Livers are sometimes worth saving.

Swim Bladders

These rubbery tubes don't look like they are worth much. They fill with gas—oxygen for deepwater fish and normal air for fish that swim near the surface—and fish use them to control the depth at which they swim. Swim bladders are actually a forerunner of lungs, which developed once fish were ready to evolve into land-based animals. They also help with sound reception, which is why they are popularly known as sounds.

The bladder of a small fish is an unappealing little rubbery thing the size of a pencil stub. The bladders of large fish are preferred for eating. Chefs want bladders that can be sliced up and used for soups and stews. In past centuries, when cod commonly grew to four and five feet long, cod sounds were popular.

This is a recipe for broiled cod sounds from 1826, found in *The Cook and Housewife's Manual*, by the Scottish writer Margaret Dods (the pen name of the outspoken feminist Christian Isobel Johnstone).

> *Clean and scald them with very hot water and rub them with salt. Take off the sloughy* [slimy] *coat, parboil them, then flour and broil them till done. Dish them, and pour a sauce made of browned gravy, pepper, cayenne, salt, a little butter kneaded in brown flour, a teaspoonful of made mustard, one of soy.*

This is an excellent recipe if you have a good day and catch a number of larger fish. They don't have to be cod. Most fish have these bladders. I don't know what happened to the bladder of the capitaine whose head I ate in Dakar, but it was a Nile perch, and Nile perch bladders are said to sell for as high as a thousand dollars.

Similarly, totoaba, a large drum fish found in the deep water of Mexico's Gulf of California, is being overfished for its sounds. Totoaba sounds can sell for thousands of dollars a pound. But it should be remembered that sounds do not weigh very much, and a pound of sounds is a large amount. It only takes about two ounces to make soup for a family.

In Asia, bladders, known as maws, are prized, especially in China. Maw soup is a Chinese delicacy. To make the soup, soak the bladder for a day, then boil it for five minutes with slices of fresh ginger. Slice it up, removing any hard parts. Simmer in a broth with shiitake mushrooms and ginger. Add a touch of cornstarch for thickening.

A gill net with salmon stuck in it is irresistible to seals. Seals sometimes get to the catch before it can be hauled in.

A school of fish will try to swim through a gill net and get stuck halfway through, caught by the gills. The seals swim from one helpless fish to the next, biting out their bellies.

Because seals are federally protected, there's not much fishers can do once seals go for their catch.

WHAT MOST PEOPLE WANT TO EAT

Lots of people (especially in the US) don't want to eat heads, livers, or any of the other stuff that I'm into that they're unfamiliar with. They just want a piece of fish, easy to eat with no bones. In deference to popular taste, that is what most fish shops and many restaurants provide.

The word *filet* probably referred to meat before it was borrowed by fishmongers. It is a French word meaning "string" or "ribbon," and meat filets were commonly tied up. Perhaps fish were, too, but they aren't now. A great deal of fish is sold commercially in filets, and it was a revolution in the early twentieth century when processors developed fast fileting machines to replace laborers, usually women.

A filet is a piece of meat sliced lengthwise from the side of the fish, parallel to the spine. To cut one you need a fileting knife, sharp, with a thin, curved blade. When you gutted the fish you made the ventral—belly—cut. Now slice the fish vertically behind the head, cutting up, from behind the gills to the fish's back, so you can then pivot the knife to cut along the spine. Halfway down you'll have passed the ribs, and you can run your knife blade flush along the backbone, pushing it all the way through to the tail. Make a cut to sever the meat from the tail. Turn the fish over and repeat for the other side, which should be easier because you can better see what you are doing.

Some fish are more difficult to filet than others because they have finer bones. A pike, a great fish to fish for and a lovely fish to eat, is very difficult to filet. Trout are a little difficult because their ribs are so fine. But why filet a trout, anyway? It cooks so well whole.

Fileting is really for larger fish. Anything small is better cooked whole, because fish is more flavorful sealed in its skin. The more you expose the meat, the less quality it has, which is why fileting is preferable to slicing in steaks. This is particularly true with fish such as salmon, which have great-flavored skin.

If you are going to take a fish from its watery home and kill it, use as much as you can. After you filet the fish, do not throw the rest away. It will make an excellent stock for a soup or stew.

After you filet, inspect the fish with a pair of tweezers and pull out any stray bones you may have missed. There will almost always be one more.

Every time she served fish my mother announced, "Careful, this is fish, and it may have bones." She was right. If making fish for the family, give the tail piece to the youngest because it will not have bones. It may also be the best piece.

HOW TO COOK A FISH

Now you have a whole fish, scaled and gutted, or a nicely cut filet. There are eight basic techniques for serving fish: Grill it, broil it, bake or roast it, sauté it, poach it, fry it, stew it, or eat it raw.

Grilled

If you are camping on a fishing trip, the easiest way to prepare your fish is to throw it on the fire and sprinkle on some salt. If the fish is whole, give it just a few minutes on each side, or five to six minutes skin side down if it's a filet.

Indigenous peoples of the Pacific Northwest, especially the Nez Perce, Yakama, and Umatilla, have a tradition of grilling salmon on a cedar plank.

A fish caught and bled a few hours before and grilled on a hot fire may be the best-cooked fish you will ever have. At home I sometimes use a stovetop grill to achieve the same pleasure.

Broiled

Sliding a fish under a broiler set at 500°F (260°C) with salt and a few herbs or spices is also a fine dish prepared in just a few minutes. Skin side up if you like to eat skin, and especially for salmon.

Sautéed

When fly fishing for trout, Ernest Hemingway brought along a skillet and butter. Hemingway took butter with him camping? For such a notable outdoorsman, it seems a very citified thing to do. Oh well, he liked his fish sautéed.

If you want to sauté fish, it is good to first dredge it in flour. This creates a buttery, browned crust that seals in

the juices. It's the standard way to cook flatfish like sole and flounder because a thin filet is perfectly done by the time the crust is browned. Throw some salt, pepper, and chopped parsley or herbs into the dredging flour if you want. To maintain the delicate sweetness of the flesh, sauté just long enough to brown the flour coating.

Baked or Roasted

A large fish can be baked for a feast. This works well with striped bass, salmon, turbot, and halibut. And it's what my Senegalese hosts did with the capitaine, mentioned previously.

Baked fish is sometimes called roasted fish, but fish is rarely roasted. The word *roast* implies rotating, or turning on a spit. Baked fish are not rotated. We save that for pigs and chickens. Baked fish are sometimes stuffed with breadcrumbs and sometimes with crustaceans or mollusks. But a well-baked fish is so glorious, it doesn't really need such embellishments. Beware of overbaking; that is the only way to go wrong with this technique. Actually, that's true of all of the techniques. Err the other way. Be vigilant. At the split second the fish is cooked, remove it from the heat.

Fried

Deep-fried fish is a strong tradition in many countries and cultures. Many Native Americans have a tradition of frying fish. The Ojibwe, or Chippewa, traditionally make cakes of perch or other flaked freshwater fish and fry them in oil. Italians serve a platter of whole tiny fried fish called fritto misto di mare or frittura di paranza. In England cod is battered and deep-fried for fish and chips. Traditionally the dish is sprinkled with vinegar, a custom that dates back to Apicius, who wrote about fried fish in the first century, saying, "Immediately after they are fried, pour hot vinegar over them." In Scotland haddock gets the same treatment. In America there is a folk custom of "fish fries" on Fridays, particularly for Catholics during the Lenten season. (The Catholic Church no longer requires its members to abstain from eating meat on Fridays, but the tradition of eating fish endures.) In the South, fish fries are often held in large halls, with local fish such as bream, bass, and catfish. Fish fries are also popular in the Midwest and especially in Wisconsin, where freshwater fish such as pike, perch, and smelt are prized. Most American fish fries use a batter made with cornmeal and eggs.

The Japanese fry fish in a batter made with egg yolks folded with beaten egg whites and wheat flour. White fish such as whiting and goby (small, white-fleshed fish from brackish waters) are often used. Americans, rather than using a batter, sometimes bread the fish—dredging it in flour, dipping it in beaten eggs, then covering it with breadcrumbs.

The Chinese are very exacting about frying. Fish is generally put in a wok with very hot oil. Frying experts master the craft of houhuo, which is knowing the exact time of frying to the second.

Squirreled fish from Jiangsu—a highly developed province of Eastern China near urban Shanghai, with picturesque canals and elaborate cuisine—is a showpiece of Chinese cooking, proudly served to Richard Nixon on his historic visit in 1972. It is a leading example of not only houhuo but daogong, the masterful handling of knives.

The fish is a lake perch, which is common in lakes all over the world and popular for baitfishing or spin casting from a small boat. The fish is scaled and gutted, and the head is cut off. Instead of removing the flesh from the bones, the bones are removed from the flesh, and the two remaining filets stay attached to the tail. This is only the beginning of the knife skill. The fish must be scored in elaborate angular cuts. It is then coated with egg yolks beaten with rice wine and dredged in cornstarch, so that when it is dipped in hot oil at just the right temperature, it suddenly puffs out, resembling the shape of a squirrel tail. It is served with the fried head placed at the front of the fish and the whole dish anointed with a sweet-and-sour sauce. It was a favorite moment in Taiwan cooking star Fu Pei-mie's popular television show, *Fu Pie-mie Time*—holding the fish by the tail, dipping it in, and *puff*.

You don't need to be a master of houhuo to make a good fried fish. There are only a few rules to the whole affair. One: Fresh fish fries better than frozen, which stores up moisture—the ideal time for frying is just after the fish has been caught. Two: The cooking oil must be very hot. Three: The fish must be cooked fast. Four: The fried fish must be eaten while still hot. If you follow these rules, fried fish is superb. If not, the fish died in vain.

Poached

While frying is fast and hot, poaching is slow and cool. It is for purists who want cooking to interfere as little as possible with the natural properties of fish. The fish—either whole or a filet—is placed in a bain-marie (a small pan of water set inside a larger pan of water). The water in the large pan simmers, while the water in the inner pan—which has the fish—quivers. Cook for a few minutes if the fish is small and thin, longer if it's fat. Eventually it will change color, stiffen. It is critical that the heat be moderate. Boiling will ruin the fish.

In the French Caribbean, fish and other seafood is poached in water with white and green onions, garlic, a pinch of salt, a sprig of thyme, some lime juice, and a small, sliced hot pepper. It is eaten as soup, and the dish is called a *blaff*. A blaff of sea urchins is my nomination for the best dish in the Caribbean.

Poached fish, simple and pure, is often a good candidate for a sauce. Sauces were frequently devised to cover up a fish that was not so fresh. But a fine poached fish sometimes deserves a well-made sauce.

Nantua sauce is a star with poached fish. The sauce comes from Ain, a mountainous area in central France, and celebrates crayfish, which are plentiful in the region. Sometimes in America it is easier to substitute lobster. This is how to make a simplified modern version:

Sauté pieces of crayfish or lobster meat with minced onions, and flame with a stiff shot of cognac. Add cream and cook until thickened. Strain out the crawfish and lobster, and put the sauce back on the stove to thicken over a low flame; it will condense. Beat in crayfish or lobster butter (made by cooking the shells of these animals in melted butter that is then chilled). You can add back the pieces of lobster or crayfish meat or keep it a smooth sauce. This is a shortcut from French classical cuisine, where a sauce takes many hours, and therefore is probably a travesty. But hardly anyone cooks that way anymore, and this works.

My favorite poached fish is a whole poached trout that is then chilled while I make a lime mayonnaise. A food processor is an excellent mayonnaise maker. Mayonnaise has to be made in just the right order—egg yolks, acid, oil—or it's a muddled mess. Beat the yolks and add fresh-squeezed lime juice and a little zest. Then, while beating, add oil very slowly, a drop at a time. Don't hurry. The trout will wait.

Soup

You can always toss fish in a pot and make a soup or stew. Soups tend to be local specialties. A bouillabaisse is a soup with the fish and mollusks of Marseille's Mediterranean waters. New Englanders make cod chowder. In New Orleans, gumbo is made with local crab, shrimp, and oysters. In San Francisco, cioppino is made with local fish, squid, crab, and mollusks. Local grouper or red snapper are used for Mexican fish soup. The Japanese use tuna for a brothy delicately seasoned soup. In the Chinese province of Hainan there is fish-lip soup (which is a bit of a mistranslation, as the "lips" are actually small strips of the skin of a shark that is becoming too endangered to feel good about eating). And in County Tyrone in Northern Ireland, they make a chive and cream soup with the funny little bottom feeders called grunts (named for the sound made with their teeth).

France famously has a soupe de poisson, a smooth, richly flavored, brick-red seafood soup. The difficulty with this soup is not the preparation but the acquisition of a good variety of fresh fish. Jean-Claude Goumard, a Breton famous as a leading Paris seafood chef, said that for soupe de poisson he liked to use whiting, red gurnard (grondin), John Dory, scorpion fish, skate, rockfish, wrasse, and more. The secret is a wide variety. Goumard said that you should just choose whatever looks good in the market and suits your taste. But he lived in Paris. You need a good market, or an exceptional day of fishing. Alternatively, ask a bottom dragger captain you know to save you some "trash fish species." Any good drag will pick up an assortment of "unwanted" fish that could work well. (That is what is wrong with bottom dragging!) Or if you go fishing and catch a bunch of weird stuff, run home and make soup.

A good fish market should have three or four fish that you like. Skip the dark oily ones, unless you caught and bled them yourself. Since you want to use three to five whole fish, you don't want large fish; and since you are going to cook them beyond recognition and grind them up, you don't want to use expensive, fine fish.

To make a soupe de poisson, throw chopped onions in hot olive oil. Add chopped garlic. Peel and seed a few tomatoes. Put these ingredients in a casserole and add a rib of chopped celery, a piece of chopped fennel, parsley, and thyme. Tuck in the selection of fresh fish, cover with water, and add a few strands of saffron. Simmer below boiling for about half an hour. Bones and heads will easily fall away at this point. They have done their job. Discard them.

Cool off the soup and run it through a food processor until it is a thick purée. Put it back in the casserole and reheat. Serve with toasted rounds of bread floating in the soup bowls with a sauce called rouille dolloped on top. Rouille is a homemade mayonnaise of beaten egg yolks, garlic, saffron powder, a small pinch of chili powder, a few squeezes of fresh lemon juice, and oil beaten in a drop at a time.

Raw

Fish can be eaten raw. This requires the best and freshest fish. Fresh fish has a supple firmness and does not smell fishy. Buy it from a reliable source or, if you are using your own caught fish, examine carefully for white parasitic worms. Fish processers place raw filets on a light table to identify and remove tiny worms with tweezers. You can do the same or do what sushi chefs do—freeze it first, quickly, at a very low temperature.

Now that I have completely disgusted you, there are many great ways of eating raw fish. The most famous raw fish is Japanese sushi, which is not as simple as just serving uncooked fish. Sushi requires knife skills for slicing with sensitivity to the grain of the fish, as well as proper brining that is subtle enough that the fish is not salty. Brining makes raw fish safer. Most raw fish dishes are in some way marinated, which is a chemical process with effects much like cooking.

Another raw fish dish that has become popular internationally—this one simple to make—is ceviche. Ceviche was invented by a people in the north of Peru, the Moche, probably in the first century. The Moche were an advanced civilization known for their pyramids and other architecture, murals, pottery, other decorative art, and sophisticated agricultural techniques.

The original Moche ceviche has since been Hispanicized, swapping in lime juice for fermented passionfruit.

The fish—usually one with tender white flesh—is immersed in the lime juice with a touch of salt and the local ají pepper (similar to habanero) and a small amount of onion. (Mexican recipes use cilantro, and less onion.) Authentic Peruvian ceviche is served only minutes after the lime juice is added. Other versions marinate longer. Scallops work well with this recipe, too.

Poke is a Hawaiian variation on a similar idea. It's usually made with high-quality tuna that has been cut into large cubes and put in a container with lightly toasted sesame seeds, chopped scallions, a little cayenne pepper powder, a couple of teaspoons of toasted sesame oil, and soy sauce. This mix is then placed in the refrigerator for a few hours or even overnight. Sometimes octopus is swapped in for the tuna.

If poke is for big fish, lomilomi iʻa is a popular way to eat small raw fish in Hawaii. The name translates as "massaged fish," because in its earliest incarnation it was rubbed with salt and spices. Traditionally it is made with small opelu fish. The scales are small and come off easily. Gut the fish and split it from the chin down the belly to the tail. Then spread it open and remove all the organs, the bones, and the gills (remember to save these spines for frying in coconut oil; see page 107).

Fill the gutted fish with limu kohu, a popular edible seaweed, cooked candlenut kernels (sold as kukui), minced onions, and tomatoes. Fold the fish over tail to head and refrigerate overnight. Open and eat.

CATCHING A SALT FISH

Okay, you are not going to catch a salted fish, though there were such myths in the Middle Ages. This was because salt fish was the only fish many inland people ever saw. There was no way to keep fish fresh for a journey.

Even in this modern age of refrigeration, you might want to preserve a fish sometime. If you like lox, you understand why.

Because of other preservation techniques like canning and freezing, we don't need to salt fish anymore—just like we don't need to preserve pork by making ham or bacon, which are also salt cured. We just like them.

There are numerous salt-based techniques that we continue to use, although they are not necessary.

Pickling

Herring, lively little devils scooped up by the netful, are candidates for pickling, as they don't stay fresh for very long. To pickle, prepare a salt brine and leave the cleaned fish in it for about a day. Then boil water with sugar, vinegar, onions, and whatever spices you like, such as black pepper, mace, mustard, bay leaves, cloves, and lemon. Let that concoction cool, then put it in a jar with the herring. Close the jar, sealing it in a bath of boiling water, place it in the refrigerator, and that fish will keep for at least a year if the jar is not opened.

Smoking

Many New England sportfishers have purchased small portable smokers for all the bluefish they love catching but don't really want to eat. Smoked bluefish on crackers is a favorite New England appetizer. For a similar reason, smoked marlin is popular in the Caribbean—people love to catch it but don't really want to eat it.

To smoke bluefish, first filet it—it's one of those smaller, not easily filleted fish. Then boil a brine with salt, sugar, and spices. Cool it off and pour it on the fish in a pan. Let the filets marinate for five or six hours, and then put them on a rack for about 24 hours to dry out. Cook them on low heat in a smoker for a few hours. (Smoking slowly is best.) This fish is delicious in spreads, dips, and pâtés.

Alaskan Natives, such as the Dena'ina and other Athabascan groups, slowly smoke salmon during the summer to eat in the offseason, and if you can get some of this fish, it is a rare treat.

Strips of sockeye salmon are hung to cure in a Dena'ina summer smokehouse in Bristol Bay, Alaska.

In Hawaii, lomilomi salmon, named after lomilomi i'a but completely different, is a popular appetizer. The salmon is covered in sea salt, wrapped, refrigerated for three days, and then washed off. Dice it and mix with diced tomatoes, onions, and green onions—all about the same size. There is no salmon in Hawaiian waters, but there is a long tradition of acquiring it from passing ships.

Salting

Salt cod is neither convenient nor pleasant to make. Cod is not a great sporting fish, and salting it requires time and space and is very smelly. With the advent of refrigeration it is also no longer necessary. You used to be able to locate a harbor used for salting fish from miles away by the smell. Upscale Manchester-by-the-Sea in Massachusetts liked to call neighboring Gloucester, where fish were cured, Gloucester-by-the-Smell. Despite its obsolescence, salt cod remains popular, though on a smaller scale, in France, Spain, Italy, Portugal, and throughout the Caribbean.

Often the salt cod sold today is just half salted, which is not as good as fully salted cod. Look for a piece that is stiff as a board, thick, and with its skin still on. It is hard to find. The best salt cod is produced in Norway, Iceland, and the Faroe Islands. It can be bought in northern Spain, Portugal, and a few other places, but the really good stuff is hard to find in the US. I sometimes bring it back from Basque country in my suitcase, but not a family suitcase, because the family objects to the fishy aroma. The smell seems to discourage customs inspectors, a benefit of traveling with salt cod, I think.

To eat your thick, hard salt fish, you must remove the salt and restore it to a fishlike texture. This is done by soaking the fish for many hours in running water so the water surrounding the fish is always fresh. In earlier times, the French used to put it in the tank above the toilet. Perfectly sanitary, and with every flush the fish got a new dose of fresh water.

Various salt cod cultures argue about who makes the best salt cod dish, but anyone who knows anything about me would guess that I'd pick one from the Basques, a people who live in a corner of France and Spain but have their own distinct culture, a language unrelated to any other known language, and a rich and celebrated cuisine. I have spent many years writing about them. My favorite salt cod dish is called pil pil, which like many terms in the Basque language is of uncertain meaning.

To make pil pil, place a well-soaked salt cod—skin up—in an earthenware casserole. Pour ample olive oil in the casserole and add slices of garlic. Set over gentle heat. When the garlic is browned, after five or six minutes, remove it and set it aside, and then remove all of the oil and set it aside in a separate container. Keep both ingredients handy. Grab the casserole and start moving it in a circular manner so that the fish is sliding around. There are arguments about clockwise versus counterclockwise. A few drips at a time, reintroduce the warm olive oil into the casserole with the cod, slowly stirring the oil until it becomes a thick, creamy, ivory-colored sauce. It is not known why this process works. Add the garlic and a few slices of guindilla pepper, which is red but not hot.

TWO CELEBRITY FISH DISHES

Truite au bleu and blackened redfish are two fish dishes you may have heard of. While truite au bleu is a rare delicacy because of the cooking requirements, blackened redfish is only rare because it has been overfished, though it has shown signs of recovery in recent years.

Truite au Bleu

Truite au bleu is the ultimate trout dish. Not many have an opportunity to try it because it must be made with a live trout. Unless you fish by a ready campfire or have a cabin by a stream, you will only find it at a restaurant that maintains a tank of live trout for this purpose. Auguste Escoffier, a chef in the nineteenth and early twentieth centuries in London and Paris who defined what is called "modern French cuisine," wrote this:

> *To make this dish it is absolutely necessary to have live trout. Prepare and boil in a large pan a fish stock with vinegar.*
>
> *About ten minutes before the moment of serving, take the trout out of the water, whack the fish on the head, gut and clean them rapidly, then slip them*

into the boiling liquid. . . . It only takes a few minutes to cook a small trout.

Serve with hollandaise sauce or melted butter.

Try it. Escoffier was talking about a brown trout, which is the native trout of Europe. Since the British could not bear life without brown trout, which are actually quite colorful, they transplanted them wherever they went. They are now as plentiful as native trout in North America. I have never tried but I suspect that rainbows, cutthroats, and other American trout, if plunged just after death into a very hot bouillon, will also turn blue. But all these different trout are not even of the same genus, so I don't know for sure. I think it would be a great experiment for someone to travel to North America and catch every trout species and cook each immediately to see if it turns blue. Volunteers?

I have noticed that any kind of trout, when freshly caught, has a slimy skin. The slime, unique to trout, is a protection from certain bacteria and also helps the fish glide through the water. It is this unique slime that turns blue (at least with brown trout) when exposed to acid, which is why the trout has to be extremely fresh and unwashed.

Some people do not like what author Alice B. Toklas called "murder in the kitchen." Some prefer that the murder be done elsewhere. But once a fish is dead, the sooner it is cooked the better. It must have been recently killed for the skin to turn blue in the stock. Some cooks pour the hot broth over the fish to turn the skin blue before gingerly slipping it into the pot to cook briefly.

Blackened Redfish

Another celebrity fish dish is blackened redfish, which, as often happens with celebrities, comes with considerable controversy. In the 1970s red snapper was becoming dangerously overfished. Both for eating and for sportfishing, it is a popular species. A white-fleshed, red-skinned, fairly large fish, it is found off the Atlantic coast from the Carolinas, throughout the Gulf of Mexico, and down as far as Brazil. In Florida, Louisiana, and Mexico it is beloved by sportfishers and chefs. It is the staple fish of Mexico. But it began showing signs of scarcity.

By 1980 New Orleans chef Paul Prudhomme had a solution. Prudhomme was a huge man with a huge personality and tremendous charm. In addition to managing his restaurant, he hosted television shows and made Cajun cuisine famous throughout the US.

Prudhomme thought he could take the pressure off of red snapper by getting people to eat more red drum, known in New Orleans as redfish. Redfish is fun to catch but not a particularly exciting fish to eat—nowhere near the quality of red snapper. In the process of popularizing it, Prudhomme invented a new way of cooking fish.

In this technique, filets of redfish are dipped in butter, then covered with a spicy Cajun blend of garlic powder, onion powder, cayenne pepper, paprika, thyme, oregano, and white, black, and red pepper—he emptied the Cajun spice shelf. Then a cast-iron pan is heated as hot as you can make it. Add a little melted butter on the spot where the filet is placed and another sizzle of butter when the filet is flipped to the other side. It is only cooked a minute or two on each side.

The Popularization of Cajun Cuisine

Cajuns, a distinct people with their own French dialect, are the Louisiana descendants of eighteenth-century French Catholics who fled Nova Scotia. The cuisine that Prudhomme made famous is a blend of Cajun cooking and the traditions of New Orleans.

Blackened redfish became the dish to eat, not just in New Orleans but all over the country, and became scarce itself. In less than 10 years there were barely any red drum left. The commercial red drum fishery was closed down. Prudhomme, a socially conscious chef, was upset. Today blackened redfish is made with farmed redfish, but the method has become a popular style of cooking many kinds of local fish all over the country, a simple way to liven up a bland fish such as a tilapia. It seems wasteful to blacken a flavorful fish. Some chefs make blackened chicken.

THE SEA BREAM (AND MY FAVORITE RECIPE)

You are probably not surprised to learn that my favorite fish dish is Basque. This would not be a surprise to anyone in Spain, a land of fish aficionados. The Basques are known for their fish.

The fish used in this recipe is a sea bream, a besugo in Spanish or bisigua in Basque. It is a middle-size fish and a fool for spin tackle, which makes it popular with sport-fishers, and it has big eyes like a Margaret Keane portrait of a fish. It is closely related to an equally catchable American fish called a porgy. Sea bream also figure prominently in Japanese cooking.

The sea bream is an example of a fish whose flavor is too delicate to ever think about blackening. In San Sebastián, one of the world's most beautiful cities, these fish rush in on high tide. You can stand on the pavement near the beach and see them all swimming in together. Where are they going in such a hurry? They are chasing tiny bait-fish. Sea bream chase lures that imitate shrimp or squid, which often work better than bait. They can be caught from the piers in the old part of town. But some locals catch them from the downtown beach with surf casting rods.

San Sebastián, known as Donostia in Basque, has gastronomic societies dedicated to preserving local recipes.

The Perfect Sea Bream

This recipe for sea bream is from a San Sebastián society called Donosti-Gain. There are a number of fine, white-fleshed fish that are good with this preparation, but none as good as a big-eyed sea bream, an irresistible charmer.

1 beautiful sea bream

4 tablespoons vinegar

6 tablespoons olive oil

4 cloves garlic, cut in slices

2 slices guindilla pepper (the same dried, red, not-too-hot pepper used in *pil pil*)

1. Scale and gut the sea bream and put it in a casserole. Roast it well in an oven. [Author's note: Cooking fish uncovered like this will take 20 minutes in a medium oven.]
2. Put the vinegar in a skillet and turn up the heat. When the vinegar is reduced by half, add the juice that is left from the fish in the casserole and let it simmer a little.
3. In another skillet add the olive oil and the garlic, and heat. When the garlic begins to turn golden, add the guindilla and turn off the heat. Add the reduction of vinegar and fish juice.
4. Bring this liquid to a boil for 1 minute.
5. Add the liquid to the sea bream.

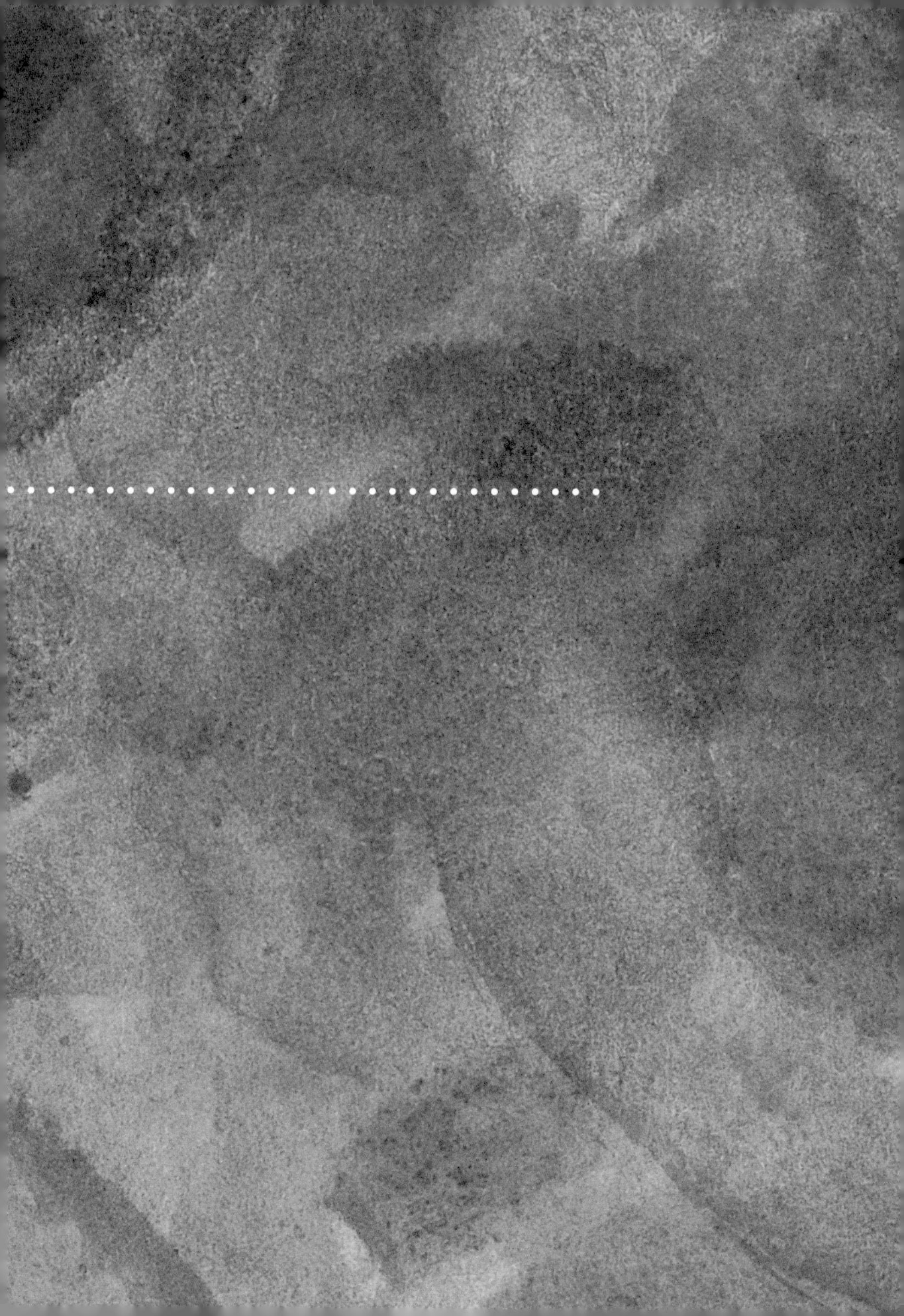

PART THREE

FISHING BY THE BOOK

If you've ever wondered why there is so much literature about fishing, you first should ask, "Why do so many writers fish?" The answer is that fishing connects you with essential elements of life. It brings you not only into the natural world but into the human world, and it raises existential questions about life and society. In Alaska, Montana, Vermont, Ireland, Scotland, Norway, Japan, and countless other places, to fish is to participate in society. And even going out on your own, you learn a lot about your world and about yourself. The reason poet Vivian Shipley gives for fishing: "I fish because the search never ends: for keys, chums, for love."

BELIEVING IN POETS

Fishing has long been a favorite topic of poets. Izaak Walton and Charles Cotton considered themselves poets first and foremost, but they also wrote what some consider an early bible of fly fishing, *The Compleat Angler*, published in 1653.

Most discussions of fishing literature begin with this book. A copy of *The Compleat Angler* sits somewhere on the shelf of many anglers, and I suspect that it often remains there untouched. The brave reader who takes it down from the shelf one rainy afternoon is in for a surprise. Like the earlier works from which it is derived, the text is a dialogue about fishing, but it also includes a sometimes disjointed compendium of three dozen poems and songs, one with music included, and many little anecdotes, some resembling jokes. Annoyingly, most of the poems are not about fishing. Why, for example, does Walton include a poem about milkmaids that is a spoof on a John Donne takeoff on a

Christopher Marlowe love poem? What do milkmaids have to do with fly fishing? I ask, and many other anglers ask the same.

Though the book is completely unoriginal and often disliked by fly fishers, maybe we are all wrong. *The Compleat Angler* is still in print and remains one of the most published books in the history of English literature. Only the Bible, *The Book of Common Prayer*, and the works of Shakespeare have been reprinted in more editions. How is this possible? It is one of those inexplicable things, like curling becoming an Olympic sport.

Fishing has been addressed by better poets than Walton. William Butler Yeats, Elizabeth Bishop, Marianne Moore, Robert Burns, John Donne, Ted Hughes—all wrote poems about fishing, as did a few New Englanders such as Robert Lowell. One of the earliest was the 1779 poem "The Fisherman" by Johann Wolfgang von Goethe:

My fish why dost thou snare,
With human wit and human guile,
Into the killing air?
Couldst see how happy fishes live
Under the stream so clear,
Thyself would plunge into the stream,
And live for ever there.

Goethe seems to question whether the fisherman appreciated the beauty of the fish's life that he was cutting short, but can we ever know for certain what Goethe was saying? Part of my problem is reading him in German, which I do because the English translators don't appear to agree. Mark Twin once wrote, "I never knew before what eternity was made for. It is to give some of us a chance to learn German."

Not surprisingly, Ireland, a land with a great love of fishing, abounds with fishing literature (also because it abounds with literature). Poets are to Ireland what cheese is to France. Some of the best fishing poems come from one of the best Irish poets.

Though he lived much of his later life in Dublin and London, where he rarely fished, Yeats grew up fishing in Sligo, which along with Mayo to the south and Donegal to the north is one of Ireland's great fishing regions. For Yeats fishing was a way of touching on landscape, culture, and love. Nostalgia for his youth is captured in vanishing herring in "The Meditation of the Old Fisherman":

The herring are not in the tides as they were of old;
My sorrow! for many a creak gave the creel in the cart
That carried the take to Sligo town to be sold,
When I was a boy with never a crack in my heart.

In 1919, at the height of the Irish struggle he supported, Yeats wrote of the simple dignity of a fly fisher in "The Fisherman," a symbol of the controlled and dignified Irishman he wished to see:

Although I can see him still—
The freckled man who goes
To a gray place on a hill
In gray Connemara clothes
At dawn to cast his flies—
It's long since I began

To call up to the eyes
This wise and simple man.

A fly fishing description leads to a song of vanishing love in "The Song of Wandering Aengus," which begins:

I went out to the hazel wood,
Because a fire was in my head,
And cut and peeled a hazel wand,
And hooked a berry to a thread;
And when white moths were on the wing,
And moth-like stars were flickering out,
I dropped the berry in a stream
And caught a little silver trout.

The poem continues into a search for a lost woman, probably Maud Gonne, actress, writer, and Irish revolutionary, whom Yeats always loved though she refused to marry him.

One of the best poems ever written about fishing is "The Fish," by Marianne Moore. As you wade through the rich imagery of this dark poem—"the / turquoise sea / of bodies"—it feels like a requiem for the fish whose harsh life and death are a metaphor for us all:

All
external
    marks of abuse are present on this
    defiant edifice—
        all the physical features of
ac-
cident—

Many essays have been written about the meaning of this poem. It is clearly about more than fishing, and it is impossible to ignore that it was written in 1918, the final year of the horrendous slaughter that we now call World War I. Most fishing stories are, on one level or another, about destruction and death, but here the metaphor is particularly powerful: This is what life is about. There is pain in every line. And while the poem can be taken as a description of the hard life at sea, Moore is clearly talking about the broader tragedy of life.

Elizabeth Bishop also wrote a poem titled "The Fish." While Bishop's poem is not as mournful as Moore's, to Bishop the fish is a tragic figure. On the surface this could be a poem about catch-and-release fishing—it is often quoted in the arguments about it. But it is also a poem about the inevitability of tragedy:

I caught a tremendous fish
and held him beside the boat
half out of water, with my hook
fast in a corner of his mouth.
He didn't fight.
He hadn't fought at all.
He hung a grunting weight,
battered and venerable
and homely . . .

The fish has scars from having been previously caught and is in pitiful condition, a victim of several attempted landings already. That triumphant moment of landing the fish turns into something pathetic:

I stared and stared
and victory filled up
the little rented boat . . .

In the end she does the only decent thing and releases the fish, a laden moment, because someone else will catch it and find even more evidence of it having been caught before.

But Bishop was not always dark. There is the lyrical "Seascape,"

where occasionally a fish jumps, like a wildflower
in an ornamental spray of spray . . .

Bishop's close friend, Robert Lowell, the opposite of Yeats in sensibility, offers the most unromantic view of fishing in "The Drunken Fisherman." Bishop and Lowell read and criticized each other's work, and Bishop's earlier poem may have influenced him, at least with the idea of fishing as a metaphor. In Lowell's poem the sad figure is the narrator, not the fish, and it is a poem about aging and facing death with disillusionment about the hollowness of his choices.

Wallowing in this bloody sty,
I cast for fish that pleased my eye
(Truly Jehovah's bow suspends
No pots of gold to weight its ends);
Only the blood-mouthed rainbow trout
Rose to my bait . . .

Lowell, a New England aristocrat, knew the culture of fly fishing. His father, also a notable poet, wrote an introduction to an edition of Walton's *Compleat Angler*. In "Fishnet," Lowell equates fishing with the process of writing and rewriting:

Yet my heart rises, I know I've gladdened a lifetime
knotting, undoing a fishnet of tarred rope;
the net will hang on the wall when the fish are eaten,
nailed like illegible bronze on the futureless future.

How could I resist a book of poetry about fishing from a contemporary poet who lives in Connecticut? In 2001 Vivian Shipley published an engaging little book titled simply *Fishing Poems*. Unlike Moore, Lowell, or Bishop, Shipley captures the joy of fishing, along with the wandering thoughts that come from it. Only a few of these 16 poems are actually about fishing in Connecticut, or even New England. In fact my favorite is "Ice Fishing in Minnesota," which I have never done. It begins wonderfully with:

You're in a walleye world if, as thoughts grow stranger
and stranger, you forget you failed basic math.

And there is "Soon, soon," rich in detail describing her young son catching a bluefish. Shipley understands fishing. In the back of *Fishing Poems* is the prose "A Woman's Guide to Salt Water Fishing," which, for men or women, is as good a fishing guide as I have ever read. She seems to be fishing in Florida since her targets are tarpon, snook, sailfish, and barracuda. We learn that tarpon, though sizable, is a woman's fish because it does not require heavy tackle. She says that a snook is "a woman's dream come true" because it is "ridiculously easy to fool," but once it hits, it's "bedlam." Sailfish, she says, follow behind "like a hyena chasing a stricken antelope. The mounting suspense is almost impossible to stand." But when they strike, Shipley cautions: "A sailfish can do strange things to otherwise normal women." The barracuda, she warns, "is formidable looking, elongated with a weird grin."

Isn't this fish writing at its best? Among her reasons for fishing, she writes, "I fish when three sons and a husband are not enough."

IT MAY BE WISDOM

Many books give advice on how to fish. Authors Lee Wulff, Ray Bergman, and Roderick Haig-Brown, in particular, have been enormously influential. Most anyone who has fished the Catskills in New York has studied Bergman. Wulff, who has written extensively about Atlantic salmon, helped popularize dry-fly fishing and the use of short fly rods. He also relentlessly developed and experimented with new flies for particular situations.

Some fishing books are more about travel than fishing, their subject being "where I have gone fishing." Novelist Thomas McGuane's fishing memoir *The Longest Silence* is a good example of this. Zane Grey, famed as an author of Western adventure novels, wrote five of the best books on fishing.

Zane Grey's fictions take place in the American West, but his nonfiction fishing tales also include the Gulf Stream, the Amazon, and the Everglades. He tells his stories well, with thoughtful messages about humankind and nature. According to Grey there are so many books about fly fishing because fly fishers are egotists. "There is some strange spell haunting stream and lake, and it persuades most anglers to have faith in experience that they think is wisdom," he wrote.

These are books for people who fish, but there is also writing about fishing that will make you want to fish even if you haven't done it before.

THE QUIET FISH

It is not an exaggeration to say that among fiction books on fly fishing, there is none better than Irishman Maurice Walsh's *Green Rushes*. When the Irish write about fly fishing, they are writing not just about a sport but about a way of life, about Irish culture. *Green Rushes* is a series of interconnected stories about people who fought in the Irish War of Independence. The most famous of the stories is "The Quiet Man," because in 1952 John Ford made it into a movie starring John Wayne and Maureen O'Hara. In the original story the main character is not as big as John Wayne, which is important because his larger brother-in-law is bullying him. The John Wayne character is an Irish-born American, but there is nothing American about the Walsh character, though he was a prizefighter in America. He returns to Ireland, not to settle down as in the movie, but to fight for Irish independence.

In the story an elite squadron of the Irish Republican Army (IRA) called the Flying Column are weary of the war, tired of the killing. As they wander around south-western Ireland, plotting attacks on the Black and Tans (assassinations, kidnappings, sabotage) and trying not to get caught, which would mean certain death, they spend a great deal of time thinking about fly fishing. This takes place in the counties of Cork and Shannon, through which the Rivers Blackwater and Shannon, two of Ireland's best salmon rivers and their tributaries, flow. The men examine every brook and river they pass for good pools to return to and fish later. Passing one such stream, a character reflects, "There would be fish in water like that, I consider lazily: speckled trout gourmandizing on the May fly, or, maybe, a clean-run salmon up from Shannon River."

But the squadron is also in an area of the most vicious fighting. The British recruits have burned the city of Cork. In one scene an IRA fighter named Owen is ordered on a mission by a superior named Hugh Forbes. "He was more intensely Republican than Hugh Forbes himself, and was afraid of nothing in this world or the next," says the narrator. And yet Owen refuses Forbes's orders. "You'll have your reasons?" asks Forbes.

"I have," says Owen. "I'm going fishing."

At times the story turns dark, but even then, there is always fishing. The narrator reflects, "Only yesterday I killed clean-run salmon down there, and now, this still summer noon, I was set to kill men—or to be killed."

In my favorite story in *Green Rushes*, "Then Came the Captain's Daughter," a British officer arrives at his wartime posting with his sister and fly-fishing tackle. He is a Scot, and some of the Flying Column fighters had fished with him in Scotland before the war. Ignoring their state of war, they all spend time fishing together. But then one day the IRA fighters realize that they have inadvertently laid out top-secret plans that were overheard by the officer and his sister. They try to make the officer promise not to reveal what he has heard, but he says he cannot do that.

What to do? The normal practice would be to shoot them both. But the fighters cannot shoot their fishing companions. Then come rumors of a settlement. The war might soon be over. The fighters take the officer and his sister to a remote spot with excellent fishing and tell them that they are prisoners who must stay there and fish until the war is over. But since, of course, they cannot be left unguarded, the fighters must take their turns fishing with them. When the war ends, Ireland is free, and so are they.

At times the story turns dark, but even then, there is always fishing.

A FAVORITE CONTEMPORARY: NORMAN MACLEAN

Norman Maclean's *A River Runs Through It* is an autobiographical novella about growing up fishing in Montana. Considered one of the most beautiful fly-fishing books, it is required reading for anyone who owns a fly

It's hard to deny the romance of casting in a Montana river.

rod. But for many years Maclean, a University of Chicago English teacher, could not find a publisher for it. Finally, in 1976, the University of Chicago Press did publish it, but few people might have ever read it were it not for Robert Redford. After considerable squabbling with Maclean, Redford got permission to turn the book into a film. By the time the film was released in 1992, Maclean had died.

The film captured the romance and mysticism of fly fishing and caused a sudden growth in the sport's popularity. Fly fishing became a fashionable thing to do. After all, people had seen Brad Pitt doing it acrobatically. I often wonder if the novices who took it up after seeing the film were disappointed once they realized that Brad

If you are a fly fisher, *A River Runs Through It* expresses better than any other story why you do it.

Pitt's extravagant rod casting—those loops and swirls back and forth over the water—is not really the way trout are caught. Fly fishing uses smaller, more precise movements, and the only time a fisher might use large, sweeping moves is when drying out a fly while dry-fly fishing. False casting, or "shadow casting," as it is called in the film, is a technique that is used at times, but it involves only one or two modest sweeps before letting go of the line. Luring a trout to rise by passing the fly back and forth over the surface of the water seldom works. It usually scares away the fish.

Both the novella and the film strike deeply into questions of why we fish and what it means. And though the story is always focused on fly fishing, it is about something much more profound. It is about the relationship between Norman Maclean, a straitlaced and responsible kid, and then man, and his wildly irresponsible brother, Paul. Yet Paul has a great saving grace: He is a superb fly fisherman, and though the two brothers are far apart in many ways, they are always close when fly fishing. Fly fishing holds this family together. The boys take a nice swipe at Izaak Walton, who they say would never have the skill to fish their river.

To the brothers and their father, fly fishing is a religion. The father is a minister, but the opening lines of the book establish that "in our family there was no clear line between religion and fly fishing." Fly fishing is what you ought to be doing, and you ought to be doing it well. You are a fly fisher or nothing. Paul theorizes, "Practically everybody on the West Coast was born in the Rocky Mountains where they failed as fly fishermen, so they migrated to the West Coast and became lawyers, certified public accountants, presidents of airline companies, gamblers, or Mormon missionaries."

If you are a fly fisher, this book expresses better than any other why you do it. If you are not a fly fisher, it explains to you what compels those who are. "I took my time walking down the trail, trying with each step to leave the world behind. Something within fishermen tries to make fishing into a world perfect and apart." There is always that moment, boots on, stepping down into the river, like slipping through a magic portal.

THAT DELICIOUS PULL

For those who fish with bait, there is Ota Pavel's *How I Came to Know Fish*. Pavel was a journalist and sportswriter from rural Czechoslovakia in what is now the Czech Republic. He and his friends fished for carp, or sometimes chub, barbell, or pike "the size of crocodiles." They used bread or dough as bait, a folk way of fishing all over the world. (In Richard Brautigan's offbeat 1967 sort-of novel, *Trout Fishing in America*, Brautigan talks about how he would take a slice of bread from breakfast and roll its soft center into balls to put on the hook. Brautigan adds, "I ended up being my own trout and eating the slice of bread myself.")

During Pavel's childhood, hungry times meant that bread would be eaten by the family, and the fish would go hungry. In better days a little anise would be added to the dough, as it was believed that the spice would attract fish.

Pavel's father was obsessed with fishing and had a pond where he bred and caught carp. Pavel caught the affliction from him. He recalls his first fish: "The rod bent into an arch and, for the first time in my life, I felt the delicious pull of a fish." If you are made to be a fisher, once you have felt that delicious pull, you never forget it. It becomes part of your muscle memory, and you crave it over and over again. And so it was with Ota Pavel.

On March 15, 1939, the Germans invaded Czechoslovakia. Pavel's mother was Christian and his father was Jewish. The father had his fish pond confiscated. "How can a Jew breed carp?" said the Germans. Then Pavel's father and two older brothers were deported to a concentration camp. Only nine-year-old Pavel and his mother remained. They had nothing to eat.

Fishing became a different endeavor, a desperate attempt to get food. Pavel made a short, sturdy fishing rod—short enough to hide under his coat, as he was not allowed to fish. The carp had become the exclusive property of the Nazis, who ate large feasts in the town's castle. Pavel studied the townspeople so he knew the informants from whom he had to hide his fishing rod, and he learned the habits of the fish warden. Then he studied the carp so he could take them quickly and efficiently. He wrote:

> *It took some time getting to know them. I had to learn to tell the difference between their bad and good moods. I had to learn to tell when they were hungry, when they were full, and when they felt like playing. I had to recognize where they were likely to swim, and where I would look for them in vain.*

Pavel's father and two brothers survived, but Pavel never lost that love of the delicious pull on his hand: "A man can look at the sky. He can stare into the forest, but nobody really sees into a river. Only with a fishing rod can one look there."

In 1973 Pavel died at the age of 42 of a heart attack. As he lay dying, he talked of dreaming of his favorite river, cupping its water in his hands and kissing it "as I would kiss a woman."

Large hungry lake carp will bite on almost anything, even a piece of bread.

Paying attention to their habits and moods is the best way to catch a fish.

BY THE BANKS OF THE TRAILER PARK

Fiction author Russell Banks is better known for describing the hardscrabble working-class lives of people in the northlands, especially northern New England, than he is for writing about fishing. But fishing is an integral part of this blue-collar northern culture, and so his characters are often seen fishing. In his story "Black Man and White Woman in Dark Green Rowboat," there is a good depiction of spin casting and the truism "but I guess it's relaxing, even if you don't catch anything."

"The Fisherman" is about ice fishing, which serves as the meticulously described background in Banks's story of Merle, an elderly man living in a trailer park and dedicated to fishing in the ice house he has carefully constructed.

Merle is not everyone's ice fisher. Though to many this is a social sport involving friends and drinking, in Banks's story it is a solitary sport. And while artificial lures are an important part of ice-fishing culture, Merle pursues perch, black bass, and bluegill with bait. He has even devised an ingenious way of spreading chum through a hole in his ice hut floor.

To his neighbors Merle is an aged oddball out in his ice house. Then he wins the lottery and has many visitors.

The story is not just about ice fishing but is a tragicomedy about life in a trailer park.

Banks also wrote "The Fish," a short story set in an unnamed Asian country that is the best spoof I know about government fishery management. The colonel in charge of a military district is concerned because his regime is Catholic and an increasing number of Buddhists are coming to the lake to worship a very large fish. This could lead to civil unrest, so the colonel decides to kill the fish. Attempts are made with machine guns and grenades, and even by mining the lake, but they all fail. And as the fish keeps surviving, its legend grows. A sample of water from the lake becomes a cherished talisman. Then the colonel decides there is money in this fish. He imposes a tax on lake water, skimming a little for himself from each sale. Eventually there is no more water in the lake, and the fish dies. The moral: If you want to kill a fish, destroy its habitat.

BIG TWO-FACED RIVER

Most people probably think of Ernest Hemingway when they think about fiction about fishing. One of his most famous books, *The Old Man and the Sea*, tells the tough-luck story of a poor Cuban fisherman. The type of commercial fishing portrayed—pursuing large fish in a small boat—is still practiced by brave and impoverished fishers in the Caribbean. But for sportsmen, the best of Hemingway's fishing writing, and really some of the best of Hemingway, is one of his early works, which introduced the reading public to an enormous talent—a two-part short story titled "Big Two-Hearted River." It was written in the 1920s, when Hemingway was still an avid fly fisherman. He had also been deeply disturbed by a brief taste of war on the Italian front in World War I.

In "Big Two-Hearted River," Nick Adams has returned weary and distressed from war and restores, almost cleanses, himself by going fishing for trout in his favorite river in the Upper Peninsula of Michigan. Similarly Hemingway came home from World War I, his leg shattered, suffering from nightmares and cold sweats, and returned to the Upper Peninsula rivers of his childhood. The story is Hemingway at his most beautiful, as it simply and gracefully describes the great curative powers of fly fishing. I am surprised that everybody didn't take up fly fishing after it was published.

Fly fishing is psychologically curative. In fact, today there are programs to take troubled combat veterans fly fishing to help them.

Nick Adams is literally, but not technically, fly fishing. He fly fishes with bait. He gathers grasshoppers, puts them in a jar that he ties around his neck, takes them out one by one to put on a hook, and casts them like artificial flies. There is an artificial fly that resembles a grasshopper, but a real grasshopper is bait.

"Big Two-Hearted River" was published in 1925, when Hemingway's first-born son, John, known as Jack, was two years old. When Jack was an adult and a renowned fly fisherman, he decided to fish his father's old rivers, including the Two Hearted River. But he found that the river was not very good for fishing, and he caught little. When he complained to his father, Papa smiled and explained that the Two Hearted had never been very good for fishing. He just loved the name.

APPENDIX:

A GUIDE FOR FISH

Ten Tips to Avoid Getting Caught

A mackerel assesses a surf casting plug.

1. Avoid eating fish that look gaudy and bright, even if this seems attractive.
2. Never eat an insect that wags its tail.
3. Never eat a fish that swims faster or slower than the fish around it.
4. Beware of two tree trunks standing next to each other in the water. See if they move.
5. You have good ears. Anglers talk a lot. Beware of strange sounds.
6. Look out for strings.
7. Bite into your food slowly. If it tastes strange, quickly spit it out.
8. If it smells good, it is fish bait.
9. If you are hooked, swim toward the angler as fast as you can instead of swimming away. It will discombobulate him.
10. If you are hooked, flip around and twist. It may be a barbless hook, in which case you can easily slip off.

BIBLIOGRAPHY

Augerot, Xanthippe. *Atlas of Pacific Salmon*. University of California Press, 2005.

Barker, Thomas. *The Art of Angling; Wherein Are Discovered Many Rare Secrets, Very Necessary to Be Knowne by All That Delight in That Recreation*. London, 1653, reprinted by Inchbold and Gawtress, 1817.

Bergman, Ray. *Trout*. Alfred A. Knopf, 1976.

Berners, Juliana. *The Treatyse of Fysshynge with an Angle*. William Pickering, 1827.

Boxberger, Daniel L. *To Fish in Common: The Ethnohistory of Lummi Indian Salmon Fishing*. University of Nebraska Press, 1989.

Carter, Jimmy. *An Outdoor Journal: Adventures and Reflections*. Bantam Books, 1988.

Cotton, Charles, and Izaac Walton. *The Compleat Angler; or, the Contemplative Man's Recreation: Being a Discourse of Fish and Fishing for the Perusal of Anglers*. Nicholas Vane, 1948.

Deloria, Vine, Jr. *Indians of the Pacific Northwest: From the Coming of the White Man to the Present Day*. Doubleday, 1977.

Dunham, Judith. *The Atlantic Salmon Fly: The Tyers and Their Art*. Chronicle Books, 1991.

Escoffier, Auguste. *Le guide culinaire: aide-mémoire de cuisine pratique*. Flammarion, 1921.

Fagan, Brian. *Fishing: How the Sea Fed Civilization*. Yale University Press, 2018.

Foggia, Lyla. *Reel Women: The World of Women Who Fish*. Three Rivers Press, 1995.

Garrison, Everett E., and Hoagy B. Carmichael. *A Master's Guide to Building a Bamboo Fly Rod: The Essential and Classic Principles and Methods*. Skyhorse, 2016.

Grey, Zane. *Tales of Fishes*. Grosset & Dunlap, 1919.

Halverson, Anders. *An Entirely Synthetic Fish: How Rainbow Trout Beguiled America and Overran the World*. Yale University Press, 2010.

Hemingway, Ernest. "Big Two-Hearted River, Part I and Part II." *The Complete Short Stories of Ernest Hemingway*. Scribner's, 1987.

Hemingway, Jack. *Misadventures of a Fly Fisherman: My Life with and Without Papa*. Taylor, 1986.

Hoffmann, Richard C. *Fishers' Craft and Lettered Art: Tracts on Fishing from the End of the Middle Ages*. University of Toronto Press, 1997.

Holden, George Parker. *The Idyl of the Split-Bamboo: A Carefully Detailed Description of the Rod's Building*. Stewart & Kidd, 1920.

Johnson, Kirk Wallace. *The Feather Thief: Beauty, Obsession, and the Natural History Heist of the Century*. Windmill Books, 2019.

Johnson, Victor R., Jr. *America's Fishing Waders: The Evolution of Modern Fishing Waders*. EP Press, 2008.

Jorgensen, Poul. *Dressing Flies for Fresh and Salt Water*. Freshet Press, 1973.

Jorgensen, Poul. *Salmon Flies: Their Character, Style, and Dressing*. Stackpole, 1978.

Kelson, George M. *The Salmon Fly: How to Dress It and How to Use It*. Wyman and Sons, Ltd., 1895.

Kurlansky, Mark. *Cod: A Biography of the Fish That Changed the World*. Walker, 1997.

Kurlansky, Mark. *Salmon: A Fish, the Earth, and the History of Their Common Fate*. Patagonia, 2020.

Kurlansky, Mark. *The Unreasonable Virtue of Fly Fishing*. Bloomsbury, 2021.

Maclean, Norman. *A River Runs Through It and Other Stories*. University of Chicago Press, 1976.

Marbury, Mary Orvis. *Favorite Flies and Their Histories*. Houghton Mifflin, 1892.

Mascall, Leonard. *A Booke of Fishing with Hooke & Line*. John Wolfe, 1590.

Pavel, Ota. *How I Came to Know Fish*, trans. Jindriska Badal and Robert McDowell. New Directions, 1990.

Pryce-Tannatt, T. E. *How To Dress Salmon Flies*. Adam and Charles Black, 1914.

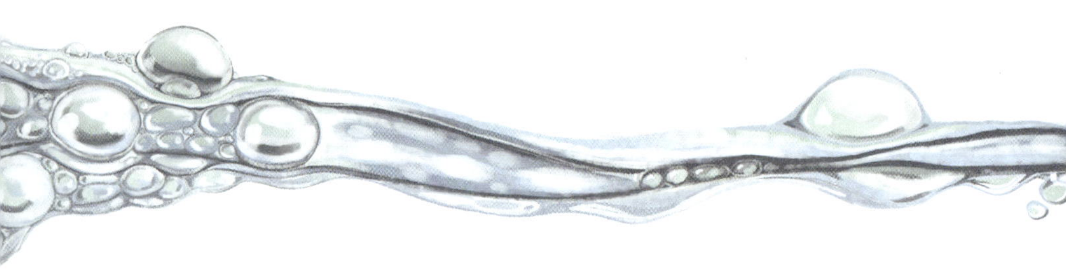

Radcliffe, William. *Fishing from the Earliest Times*. Ares, 1974.

Stewart, Hilary. *Indian Fishing: Early Methods on the Northwest Coast*. University of Washington Press, 1977.

Trench, Charles Chenevix. *A History of Angling*. Hart-Davis MacGibbon, 1974.

Walsh, Maurice. *Green Rushes*. W&R Chambers, 1935.

Walton, Izaac. *The Compleat Angler; or, the Contemplative Man's Recreation: Being a Discourse of Fish and Fishing for the Perusal of Anglers.* The Heritage Press, 1948.

Wulff, Joan Salvato. *Joan Wulff's Fly Fishing: Expert Advice from a Woman's Perspective*. Stackpole, 1991.

Wulff, Lee. *The Atlantic Salmon*. A.S. Barnes, 1958.

Wulff, Lee. *Bush Pilot Angler*. Down East Books, 2000.

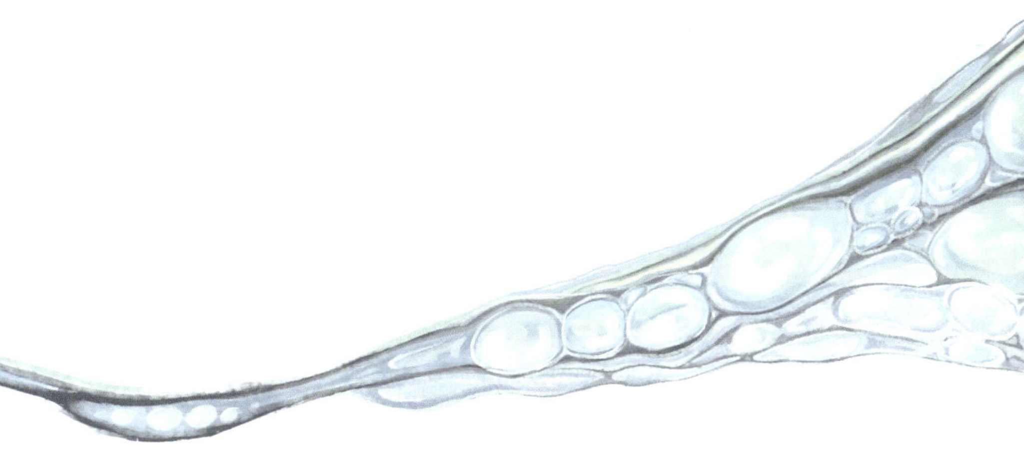

The mission of Storey Publishing is to serve our customers by publishing practical information that encourages personal independence in harmony with the environment.

Edited by Kristen Hewitt
Art direction and book design by Sophie Gerry
Illustrations by © Bri Dostie

Storey Publishing
210 MASS MoCA Way
North Adams, MA 01247
storey.com

Storey Publishing is an imprint of Workman Publishing, a division of Hachette Book Group, Inc., 1290 Avenue of the Americas, New York, NY 10104. The Storey Publishing name and logo are registered trademarks of Hachette Book Group, Inc.

ISBNs: 978-1-63586-972-9 (paper over board); 978-1-63586-973-6 (ebook)

Printed in Malaysia by R. R. Donnelley on paper from responsible sources
10 9 8 7 6 5 4 3 2 1

APS

Library of Congress Cataloging-in-Publication Data on file

ACKNOWLEDGMENTS

Thanks to my agent, Danielle Svetkov, for her ideas and energy; to Kristen Hewitt for helping me put this together; and to many people all over the world who helped teach me to be a better fisherman. These include Glenda Powell, who taught me spey rod casting on the River Blackwater in Ireland, and especially Brian Richter, who taught me so much on the rivers of central Idaho.